DAVID L. McKENNA

THE WHISPER OF HIS GRACE

When We Hurt and Ask "Why?"

WORD BOOKS
PUBLISHER
WACO, TEXAS

A DIVISION OF
WORD, INCORPORATED

THE WHISPER OF HIS GRACE

Library of Congress Cataloging in Publication Data

McKenna, David L. (David Loren), 1929–
   The whisper of his grace.

   Bibliography: p.
   1. Suffering—Religious aspects—Christianity.
I. Title.
BT732.7.M29 1987   231'.8   87-8335
ISBN 0-8499-0560-5

7898 RRD 987654321

Printed in the United States of America

To my Mother

A woman transformed
by grace—through suffering—
from a taxi dancer to a
saint of God

Contents

> Indeed these are the mere edges
> of His ways,
> And how small a whisper we hear
> of Him!
>
> Job 26:14

Author's Preface

After completing the volume on *Job* in *The Communicator's Commentary,* I was so full of my subject that I wanted to share my insights with other people. At the risk of oversimplifying one of the most profound books of the Bible, I put together a series on the Book of Job that included "How Righteousness Works, How Suffering Hurts, How Faith Grows, How God Speaks, and How Grace Transforms." The response to these messages in conferences and seminars overwhelmed me. In more than thirty years of public ministry, I had never struck such a responsive chord of human need. People literally swamped me with questions that revealed the intriguing nature of the Book of Job as well as the nagging reality of their own suffering.

Then and there, I decided that I would write a sequel to this commentary—smaller, less formal, and more personalized. The real difference between the two books, however, is found in the beginning and ending. The commentary begins with the introduction of Job, the perfect man. This book begins with the human questions that all who suffer will ask, "Why me? Why this? Why now?" Whenever I ask these questions in a public setting, heads nod and eyes light up. Whatever the circumstances of our suffering—physical, emotional, intellectual, social, or spiritual—the questions are the same. While Job may be too perfect for us in his righteous-ness, we immediately identify with him when he suffers and screams "*Why?*" Here we stand on common ground with all humanity. Here this book begins.

After I finished writing the commentary on *Job* I could not wait to tell people about the ending. While on a safari in Africa, I met a woman who was teaching a Bible class on the Book of Job. Late into the night, we sat on the veranda watch-ing the shadowy forms of animals come and go as we talked about the prophetic leaning of Job's story toward the grace of Jesus Christ. Before we talked, she intended to follow the scholars' advice and eliminate the Epilogue which tells of Job's restoration. "No, no," I remember pleading with her. "Don't leave him on the ashheap. Without the Epilogue, we do not understand the inspired message of the Book of Job. Although it begins with the question of justice, it ends as a beautiful story of grace."

Our conversation led me to the title for this book. Most of us read the Book of Job thinking that we will find the answer to the question, "Why do the innocent suffer?" This is the question of God's justice, legitimate to be sure, but never answered to our full satisfaction. In the Book of Job, God asks us the prior question about Himself, "Who am I?" As a righteous, rich, and famous man, Job knew God in His power, wisdom, and justice. But until he suffered, he did not know Him as the God of grace. Yet he had the hint when he sang of God's majesty,

> Indeed these are the mere edges
> of His ways,
> And how small a whisper we hear
> of Him!
> But the thunder of His power
> who can understand?
> (Job 26:14)

Grace is a small whisper. Like an intimate word between two lovers, it is God's way of saying, "I love you." This is the message of Job for all who suffer and ask "*Why?*" God will answer with *The Whisper of His Grace.*

Writing a book is an experience of grace itself. Even now my wife Janet sits downstairs during the weekend hours that should belong exclusively to her. Instead, she graciously shares her time with a word processor and a manuscript. In the same sequence, the staff of the President's office at Asbury Theological Seminary stands on call waiting for me to finish a chapter, review the copy, and interpret my infamous scribbling. As my editor and Executive Assistant, Sheila Lovell is personally acquainted with the meaning of every metaphor and the placement of every comma in the Book of Job. Lois Mulcahy, my secretary, knows the Book better than I do. In preparation for putting *The Whisper of His Grace* on the word processor, she made the Book of Job the subject of her own personal Bible study. More than once, she urged me to make the text more meaningful for those who suffer. Hour after hour, she sat at the computer until the manuscript met her standard of perfection. To Janet, Sheila, and Lois, thank you for your gift of grace to me—a whisper to be sure, but clear to all who hear.

THE
WHISPER
OF HIS
GRACE

1
When We Ask "Why?"

Sooner or later each of us suffers. When we do, we all ask the same three questions:

Why me?
Why this?
Why now?

If we look and listen, we see and hear these questions being asked all around us:

• On the day of his retirement dinner, the vice-president of a corporation is informed that he has cancer. With the anticipation of travel and leisure usurped by emergency surgery, who can blame him if he asks, "Why me? Why this? Why now?"

• A young woman who has sacrificed her career with a major accounting firm to work for a pittance in a Christian organization is informed that she must resign her job and change climates because she has multiple sclerosis. As she gives her last timely and accurate report on finances, her enthusiasm overrides the questions through which she is working, "Why me? Why this? Why now?"

• Ten days before graduation from seminary a thirty-

15

year-old student, his wife, and baby are confronted head-on
by a loaded gravel truck that swerves into their lane. Spin-
ning the wheel to save his wife and baby, Tom receives the
full blow of the crash. A crushed head and a broken body
threaten his life, his mind, and his ministry. While waiting
and praying in the emergency room that night, we ask his
questions for him, "Why me? Why this? Why now?"

• A brilliant international student is accepted for doc-
toral study at Harvard. Coincidentally, his sponsor informs
him that he can no longer give him financial assistance.
Restrictions on his student visa force him to do menial work
at minimum wage and he cannot even support his wife
and baby. All of his dreams collapse under demands for tu-
ition payment and the approaching deadline on his visa. The
loss of face is more than he can bear. Just short of self-
destruction, he sinks into severe depression, physical exhaustion, and spiritual bitterness. In counsel with me he asks,
"Why me? Why this? Why now?"

• An executive of a Christian publishing company is
heading home with his son on Christmas Day. Along the
road they spot a hitch-hiker whom they had seen thumbing a
ride in the same place the day before. Compassion mingled
with curiosity causes the driver to stop and ask if the man
needs help. The story is poured out of a jobless, penniless,
hungry, and helpless hitch-hiker, trying to get back home on
Christmas Day. Despite the interruption to the Christmas
plans for his family, the executive takes him home, feeds him,
clothes him, and lets him share as they open their gifts
around the fireplace. Waiting until the last minute, the modern Good Samaritan gives money to the man whom he found
alongside the road and hurries him to catch the only bus that
will take him home on Christmas Day. In their haste, they
dampen the coals from the fireplace and put them in a trash
can in the breezeway between the house and the garage
along with the wadded wrappings from their gifts. Moments
later, the wife smells smoke, opens the kitchen door, and is
driven back by a wind-whipped wall of flames. While he is on
a mission of mercy, the executive's home burns to the ground
and everything is lost. Who can blame the son who asked his

father if he understands the economy of God? Honesty causes the executive to shake his head "No." Together, they ask, "Why us? Why this? Why now?"

• A well-to-do financier reflects on the question, "Why do bad things happen to good people?" Thieves have robbed his home and escaped with his wife's jewels. In full seriousness he reasons, "I work hard, try to be good . . . and then this happens. I just don't understand it . . . and to tell you the truth, I'm bitter." Even the suffering of lost luxury provokes the question, "Why me? Why this? Why now?"

Only human beings can ask *"Why?"* Created in the image of God, it is our nature to reflect upon our suffering, put it into the perspective of experience, and pose questions that probe into the very heart of human existence. In truth our question goes deeper than our God-given nature. Intentionally or not, when we ask "Why?", we also challenge the nature of God—His justice, His wisdom, and His power.

Why Me?

No matter *who* we are, saint or sinner, when we suffer our first question is, "Why me?" To whom do we cry? Unless it is a meaningless shout to the four winds, the object of our cry is God Himself. Whether we are victims or culprits, innocent or guilty, we feel as if our suffering is unfair. When an innocent two-year-old child is stricken with leukemia, we ask, "Why her?" But we cannot forget that a seventy-year-old man who is dying of lung cancer caused by smoking two packs of cigarettes a day for more than fifty years will also ask the question, "Why me?" After all, thousands of two-pack-a-day seventy-year-olds are still alive and free from cancer. Therefore, "Why me?" is a question that we ask no matter who we are. Whether the cause of our pain is unknown, self-imposed, accidental, or deliberate, we believe that we have been singled out to suffer. Furthermore, we refuse to believe that we are victims of a cruel trick of chance. "Why me?" is a cry that questions the justice of God. We believe that our suffering is *unfair*.

Why This?

No matter *what* we suffer, we also ask, "Why this?" Another gift of our divine creation is the ability to perceive ourselves as distinctive individuals. We transfer that same perception to our suffering. Even though millions of others may develop the same disease, face the same pain, or sense the same anguish, our suffering is *unique*.

Six weeks after my sixty-nine-year-old father passed a medical exam without a trace of problems, a massive heart attack and eleven minutes without oxygen left him a vegetable. When my sister arrived at the hospital room, the attending physician met her at the door with the frightful warning, "If this man has a son, warn him that this kind of heart attack is hereditary." Heeding his warning, I have become a jogger on a self-imposed regimen of periodic treadmill tests. The doctor has complimented me for having the heart of a twenty-year-old and yet the specter of heredity hangs over me. If it happens, I will still ask, "Why this?"

The truth of the matter is that we cannot understand why, of all the kinds of suffering, we are victimized by one particular kind. Again, "Why this?" is an implied threat that God doesn't know what He is doing. If He were wise as well as just, He would have chosen for us a more tolerable kind of suffering. Whatever we suffer, it is unique.

Why Now?

No matter *when* we suffer, we ask "Why now?" Only human beings are endowed with a sense of continuity in time that extends into eternity. Not only can we remember our past, but we can anticipate the future. Perhaps that is why suffering is always *untimely*. To be human is to have plans for the future. Not even the most glorious memories of the past can compensate for the disruption of dreams about tomorrow. My ninety-year-old mother-in-law is in a nursing home. Senility has robbed her of most mental functions, except that she still anticipates her meals. For illness to disrupt Mom's meals is as upsetting to her as it is to the person whose plans for world travel and retirement are quashed by cancer. Whether young, middle-aged, or old, when suffering comes we ask, "Why now?" Behind our question is the hidden fear that God may not be fully in control. *If He really cares for us*, we think to ourselves, *why doesn't He arrange a more convenient time for bad things to happen to us?*

Few of us have the perspective of Jim True, the owner of the racing car which Bobby Rahal drove to victory in the Indianapolis 500 in 1986. Jim was in the last stages of virulent cancer at the time of the race. Reporters asked him how he responded to the prospect of imminent death. Jim True answered, "My goals haven't changed; only my time schedule." A more typical answer, at least when our problems first arise, is to ask with furrowed brow, "Why now?"

Our personal suffering, then, is always unfair, unique, and untimely. Our questions, "Why me? Why this? Why now?" arise naturally out of our humanity as challenges to the justice, wisdom, and power of God. In other words, suffering takes us to the outer edges of our faith, where contradiction gives us the option of growing in grace or festering in bitterness.

Job: Symbol of Suffering

Job is the person with whom we identify in suffering. When calamity after calamity strikes him down, he dares to ask a silent and hidden God, "Why me? Why this? Why now?" His questions push him to the frontiers of his faith where he confronts contradictions that he cannot handle. Bordering on blasphemy, Job questions the justice, wisdom, and power of God whom he both fears and trusts.

The outcome of Job's painful pilgrimage through suffering is a surprise. As I told the financier who asked if I had an answer to his question about bad things happening to good people, "Yes, God has an answer in Job. It may not be the one we want, but it is the one we need."

Job's journey through suffering has even more surprises in store for us. At its extreme, Job's suffering is partial and limited. He stands on the threshold of death, but never steps through the door. He is abandoned by friends, but never quite alone. He is almost forsaken by God, but finally hears His voice. From a human standpoint this is as far as we can go in understanding the meaning of suffering. Only someone who has experienced the ultimate suffering—in the fangs of death, without human support and forsaken by God—can fully assure us of knowing and feeling whatever anguish or pain we are going through. Jesus Christ is that person. With us, He experienced physical, mental, and emotional suffering. He, too, asked the human questions, "Why me? Why this? Why now?" But He and He alone went through ultimate suffering—abandoned by friends, forsaken by God, victimized by death, and assaulted by hell. In that sense, none of us can fully identify with Him as we can with Job. Yet because of Him we have the confidence that He knows and feels our suffering, whatever it may be.

Our journey with Job must always be taken with our mind's eye looking forward. The more we study the Book of Job the more we sense that the story leans into the future toward Jesus Christ—His incarnation, passion, death, resurrection, and grace. Once we read Job with that view in mind, our spirits leap forward to realize that the Book is far more than poetry at its best. It is prophecy at its peak. So with our fellow sufferers, Job and Jesus, we dare ask, "Why me? Why this? Why now?"

2

How Righteousness Works

If anyone who suffers has the right to ask, "Why me?" it
is Job. In the biblical book that bears his name he is introduced to us as a person who is "perfect" in righteousness.
This does not mean that Job is sinless. Jesus is the only human
being who can make that claim. "Perfect" in this sense means
that his righteousness permeates every relationship of his life
as his working principle. After all, righteousness is a matter
of relationships—with God, with things, and with other people. The biblical definition of righteousness involves each of
these three relationships. In one instance the word means
being right; in another it is used to mean *doing right*; in still
another case it means *putting right*. Job qualifies as a righteous person on each of these counts, so much so that he is
commended by God as "wholly righteous" or, translated into
our terms, "perfect."

While we may rebel against the thought of a person as
perfect as Job, we need to know him better if we are to
understand the meaning of suffering. As is so often the case,
we learn best from people who stand out as models. When
Job, a perfect man, suffers and cries, "Why me?" we learn

that we are neither the first to raise the question nor do we cry alone.

Being Right with God

Job is introduced to us without fanfare. Simply and emphatically his story begins with the line, "There was a man in the land of Uz. His name was Job."

Uz is a shadowy land. Although its existence is confirmed by ancient history, it is so old that it predates written records. For those of us who are living today, in an age when we are drowning in a sea of information that is instant, global, and permanent, we cannot imagine a time without written records. Instead of computer networks, signposts along caravan trails on which travelers scratched "graffiti" notes constituted the information system of Job's time. "Camel express" and a serious game of "pass it on" among strangers slowly took garbled messages across desolate stretches of land.

Imagine living in a time before God's Word was written on tablets of stone, shards of pottery, scrolls of parchment, or reams of India paper. Sitting in my study, I envisioned the shelves being emptied of all traces of God's special written revelation. Multiple versions of the Bible disappeared, expansive commentaries vanished, hundreds of Christian books evaporated, and thousands of megabytes on biblical themes were instantly erased. Momentarily transported back to the land of Uz and the time of Job, I realized how precious God's written Word is to me and how much my faith depends upon it. Alone with the vision of empty shelves, I wondered aloud, "Without the written revelation, how could Job be 'perfect' in 'righteousness'?"

The Gift of Physical Creation

Natural revelation led Job to faith in God. Fundamental to all revelation is physical *creation* itself. Ancients like Job lived close to the land and on the margins of survival. Of necessity, they paid particular attention to the cycles of the seasons, the whimsies of the weather, and the mysteries of nature. Translating their observations into a primitive theology, they envisioned the God of creation as a powerful force. Along with the heathen about whom Paul writes in Romans, the people of Uz in Job's time would be included in the truth, "For since the creation of the world His invisible *attributes* are clearly seen, being understood by the things that are made, *even* His eternal power and God-head, so that they are without excuse" (Rom. 1:20).

The Gift of Moral Law

Complementing God's creation as the ground of his faith, Job also shared with all humanity the natural gift of *moral law*. Out of the philosophy of Immanuel Kant comes his oft-quoted statement about sensing the existence of God through "the starry heavens above and the moral law within." John, in his Gospel, becomes even more specific in revealing the nature of God. He refers to the light that "gives light to every man who comes into the world" (John 1:9). Whether the reference is to the pangs of conscience, the intuitive sense of God, or the work of prevenient grace within the human heart, the "light" to which John refers is elemental, universal, and shining Godward.

Andrew Laing, the anthropologist, found a sense of God in every world culture he studied. Other anthropologists have also discovered common taboos in every culture which make violations of nature such as incest a sin and a crime. However primitive it may be, there is ingrained in every human heart a God-given standard of right and wrong, which can be cultivated for good or twisted for evil. Whatever that moral law may be, it is a complement to natural law in the development of faith and righteousness. Job is described as a person who is particularly sensitive to the moral law within as he "shunned evil" as well as "feared God."

The Gift of Natural Reason

In addition to the revealed gifts of physical creation and the moral law, Job also had the cultivated asset of *natural reason* by which he came to righteousness. Contrary to some exponents of faith, reason is not in conflict with religious belief or spiritual experience. Instead, it operates in concert with what we feel and what we do. Educators sum up the totality of human learning with the question, "How can I know what I think until I feel what I do?" Our humanity, then, gives us the capacity to reflect upon our spiritual impulses in order to explain them for ourselves and teach their meaning to others. The result is theology. So even though Job lived in a time without the special revelation of the written Word of God, he had a theology developed out of the power of creation, the moral checks of conscience, and the logical conclusions of a searching mind. As primitive as this theological system may seem, it provided Job with the basis for a personal relationship with God. Herein lies the mystery and the miracle of Job's "perfection" in righteousness.

Righteousness begins by "being right" with God and within ourselves. Job meets this qualification as a man who is described as ". . . blameless and upright . . . one who feared God and shunned evil." In a word, Job exemplifies what it means to be spiritual in person and religious in practice. A person may be religious without being spiritual, but one cannot be spiritual without being religious. Essentially spirituality is integrity of character and consistency of conduct. John Wesley preached "perfect love" as the gift of God which fills the heart and guides the behavior of the believer. For him, personal holiness and social holiness were one. Long before Wesley articulated the doctrine, however, Job lived a holy life—inside and outside, personally and socially.

Another synonym for Job's perfection in righteousness is "sincere"—a strong biblical word that means literally "without wax." The word picture comes from the marketplace in the ancient East. There alabaster pottery had to stand the test of being held up against the brilliant light of the burning sun to see if the work had any flaws that had been filled in with wax. Symbolizing the final judgment scene, no hidden flaws escaped and no cosmetic coverups succeeded. Job stood the test. Scrutinized under the laser light of God for hidden flaws in his character or inconsistencies in his conduct, he is "without wax."

Job's perfection went beyond self-perpetuating piety. He worked at righteousness by the discipline of shunning evil under the fear of God. Out of natural revelation of creation, conscience, and reason, a theological system developed called "the Wisdom School." Several books of the Bible come through the teaching of this school and are identified as "Wisdom Literature"—Job, Psalms, Proverbs, Ecclesiastes, and Song of Solomon. One sentence sums up their theology, "The fear of the Lord is the beginning of wisdom." Once again, in the word "wisdom" we meet a concept that is closely related to "perfect." Wisdom is our ability to see things whole. To the credit of the ancient scholars of the Wisdom School, they realized that a centering on God even in fear is a starting point for understanding the interlocking relationships which hold the physical universe and human society together. Accordingly, Job's righteousness worked to make him wise as well as holy.

Doing Right with Things

As the land of Uz existed before the time of the written Word, we also know that it was a land without a code of law. Ancient civilization in the Middle East centered in the land west of the Jordan River. To the east of the river only the most venturesome pioneers took the risk of making a fortune against the loneliness of the sparsely populated region, the unpredictability of the weather, and the certainty of vicious attacks by roving bands of thieves and rustlers.

Job is a rare man—one of a kind. Rather than settling for the security of civilized country, he risked his righteousness against the lawlessness of the eastern frontier. The result is another dimension of "human perfection." In counting the wealth Job accumulated, we learn that every animal he owned, every trade he plied, and every servant he hired represented the perfect empire in numbers and diversity. So much so that he earned the reputation as "the greatest of all the people of the East" (Job 1:3).

Job's reputation for righteousness is linked to his reputation for riches. In the easily overlooked word "and" (verse 2) a bridge is built between his "being right with God" *and* "doing right with things."

Righteousness and riches are not automatically connected as some current preachers seem to promise. Faith and poverty are closer companions. Yet, we cannot deny that practical righteousness has an integrity which is often rewarded, especially in secular professions, and more especially in competitive businesses that are not regulated by law. In such circumstances, the wealthiest of entrepreneurs are called "robber barons" and are subject to hate as well as fear and jealousy. Job is the exception because he became rich without compromising his integrity or ruining his reputation.

My father used to say to me, "Son, if you want to make a fortune, go into a business that is known for its dishonesty and be honest." I never tested his advice in a secular career but I have turned the thought into a working principle for my Christian witness. My testimony is most effective when I become involved in situations where Christians are not expected to be. For instance, I have never been more fully alive as a Christian than when I walked where angels feared to tread as Chairman of the Governor's Commission to study gambling in the state of Washington. The experience helped me understand the response of a persecuted Christian pastor from a communist nation who is given asylum in America. Once here, he longs for the beauty of a church purified by the fire of persecution.

Fame and fortune, however, are not the primary evidence that Job's righteousness included "doing right with things." Far more important is the fact that neither his righteousness nor riches ruined his family. In the same breath with which the author of Job describes the immense wealth and the incomparable fame of Job, he also tells how celebration characterized the life of Job's sons and daughters. What a contrast with so many wealthy families! In recent days, newspapers have headlined court battles over the control of family fortunes in which brothers and sisters fight bitterly against each other. Another headline reports a murder trial of an heir who killed his mother and brother in order to claim the family fortune for himself.

Other wealthy families pursue happiness in a celebration of decadence. Our Bluegrass region is known for its elaborate parties during the week of the Kentucky Derby. You can laugh and cry at the game of "one-upmanship" that hosting families play. Exotic themes, extravagant costumes, star-studded guest lists, and exorbitant expenditures are the competitive standards. How hollow their happiness! A few years ago a Greek magnate ran low on themes for his yacht parties while docked in Monaco. So the invitation to the guests asked them to come dressed symbolizing a movie title. When the guests arrived, they were greeted on the deck of the ship by their host, dressed in black leather, sitting on a motorcycle, with a shotgun across his lap. He represented the film *Easy Rider*.

Decadent wealth is not necessary to spoil families. In plush America psychologists have discovered a disease called "affluenza." Children from well-to-do families are afflicted by the disease. The symptoms are all the signs of poverty—depression, loneliness, exhaustion, escape, substance abuse, shoplifting, physical breakdown, and even suicide. The diagnosis is relatively simple. Affluent parents who substitute money and material things for their love and presence do irreparable damage to their children. Money can make emotional monsters and moral dwarfs of children. But it need not. Job is an exception. He practiced his religion joyfully and held his riches lightly. A family that knew how to celebrate without sin is his witness.

Not long ago, a multi-millionaire came to Christ. One day he invited me to join a small group of Christian friends to advise him on using his fortune for the glory of God. We began to think like businessmen. Our first question to our friend was, "How can you make the best investment with the highest return for the kingdom of God?" Suddenly the Spirit of God interrupted my thoughts with an insight, "We are starting with the wrong question!"

Compelled to speak, I blurted out, "What if God asks you to give it all away?" Startled by such a demanding thought, the superrich man stared straight at me while he weighed his answer. The honest smile of a new Christian broke across his face when he confessed, "I'm not that much

of a Christian . . . yet." Our conversation then returned
to the "reality" of other options and we left him to make a
decision.

Two or three days later a brief memo arrived from him
informing me of his decision. In one crisp sentence he wrote
that he no longer needed the fame and fortune on which he
had so long depended. Jesus was now his Lord as well as his
Savior. Above his signature at the end of the memo he wrote,
"Joy in His service." As with Job, he had learned how to
celebrate his wealth by "doing right with things."

Putting Right with Others

Righteousness is responsibility. "Being right with God,
doing right with things, and putting things right with others." Again, Job serves as our example for an oft-neglected
dimension of righteousness which the Bible defines as
"putting things right with others."

Returning to the shadowy land of Uz, we learn that Job
lived in a society without professional priests. The wilderness
east of the Jordan had no temples, synagogues, ceremonial
feasts, sacrificial rights, and, therefore, no need for the service of priests. Thus the burden for the spiritual life of his
family fell upon the father. Job served his family well: "Job
would send and sanctify them, and he would rise early in the
morning and offer burnt offerings. . . . For Job said, 'It
may be that my sons have sinned and cursed God in their
hearts.' Thus he did regularly" (Job 1:5).

Again, imagine yourself in a culture without priests. All
the responsibility for the spiritual development for our family
that we have turned over to the professional clergy would fall
back on us. Preaching, teaching, communion, counseling—
worship services, Sunday school, prayer meetings, Christian
school, day care centers, and summer camps. Peter Berger
and his wife have written a book on the problems created
when institutions and professionals take over the functions
primarily reserved for the family. With provocative insight
the Bergers conclude that whenever and wherever we have
turned over family functions to mediating agencies, even the

church, the problems we are trying to solve are actually aggravated. The spiritual development of the family is an example. No longer is the family the center for spiritual development through Bible study, family devotions, dinner conversation, moral discipline, and spiritual counsel. We expect religious specialists in each category to assume these responsibilities for us. The result? Too often the family has become one of the weakest links in the chain of spiritual development.

Some time ago the medical profession realized that the overemphasis on specialization had almost eliminated the role of the family doctor. To correct the imbalance, medical schools once again began to offer programs in family practice and reestablish its credibility among doctors. As a seminary president who is watching the ministry turn more and more to specialization in counseling, Christian education, evangelism, missions, urban and ethnic studies, youth and singles' ministries, or emphasis on the elderly, I often feel as if we need to reestablish the role and credibility of family ministry. Spiritual development in our homes is our most critical need today.

Job had no priest to whom he could turn in the land of Uz. Solely on his own he accepted his responsibility as father and priest for his family. The fact that his sons and daughters committed no obvious sin in their celebration is a credit to the quality of his family life (Job 1:4). Job's spiritual sensitivity, however, extends to the sins of heart—motives and intentions, lusts and loves, wishes and ambitions. For those of us who let blatant sins slip by for ourselves or our families, the perfection of Job may seem to border on the compulsive. If so, we forget that his righteousness did not create a joyless religion for his family. Their love for celebration denies such a thought. Instead, we sense that Job lives so close to God that he wanted nothing to break the fellowship for him or his family. Centuries later he would have said "Amen" to the hymn writer's verse:

> Quick as the apple of an eye,
> O God, my conscience make!
> Awake my soul, when sin is nigh,
> And keep it still awake.

Much might be made of the fact that Job regularly made priestly sacrifice for the sins of his family. The religious function, however, is secondary to the spiritual principle that Job teaches us, especially if we are parents. By offering regular sacrifices for his children, even for the secrets in their hearts, Job taught them the meaning of forgiveness. The more literal biblical interpretation of righteousness includes "putting right for others."

Of all the traits that parents instill in their children by example, forgiveness is the most difficult. Early in my career as a college president, a sophomore appeared before me as a court of last resort to appeal his dismissal from school. Violation after violation of residence hall rules had exhausted the patience of directors, deans, and disciplinary committees. His hostility knew no bounds. Whatever awe may seem to pervade a president's office had no effect on him. Anger and hatred exposed a vicious rebellion against anyone in authority. As I listened to him vent his spleen, a contradiction posed itself in my mind. His father enjoyed the reputation as one of the most powerful and effective evangelists in the church. The inconsistency snagged my thoughts. When he had finished and waited for my response, I caught him completely off guard with the unofficial question, "Have you ever been forgiven?" A slap in the face would not have been more shocking. His eyes emptied of fire, his head dropped, and he choked out a barely audible, "No."

"Would you like to be forgiven?" I asked. His answer taught me a lesson of a lifetime. Sobbing now, he lifted the lid that covered his resentment, "I have heard my father invite thousands of people to come to Christ . . . but he has never asked me if I wanted to be forgiven." We prayed . . . he stayed . . . and today he is a college president!

From that time on, I determined that my primary responsibility to my family was to teach the meaning of forgiveness. The most excruciating memories of my fatherhood are the times when I have flung a flimsy bridge across the chasm of anger, impatience, or sarcasm which alienated me from my family, walked unsteadily over that bridge, and begged for forgiveness on the other side. No words can describe the difference I feel when I read a passage of scripture on

forgiveness, sing a song in the family pew, or pray in our devotions, "Forgive us our sins." Without denying the priestly
function of a pastor, no one can substitute for the parent who
works out righteousness by "putting right" the relationship
with his or her family through the sacrifice of forgiveness.

We have now met Job, fully human as we are and yet a
person who exemplifies perfection in righteousness. At first
thought we may resent him because he appears to be too
good. But then the practicalities of his religion put righteousness within our reach. Biblically, the standard is not too
high. Righteousness means *being right, doing right,* and *putting right*. Practically, righteousness is everything we aspire
to be—consistent in character, honest in our dealings, and
responsible in our relationships.

What does all this have to do with suffering? Conclusions leap out at us. Most obvious is the fact that *suffering is no
respecter of persons*. Job's perfection in righteousness takes
away any thought that he *deserved* to suffer. Once and for all,
the idea that you can establish a direct cause-and-effect relationship between sin and suffering is refuted. Some people
may bring suffering upon themselves by sin, but there is
always the exception of the grosser sin and the contradiction
of good health, long life, and great prosperity. Therefore,
the first step toward understanding the meaning of suffering
is to cancel the notion that we can always explain it as a
consequence of sin. If we take such a position, not only do we
reject the principle that God is trying to teach us in the story
of Job, but we are hopelessly stymied by the incomparable
suffering of Jesus Christ. As the only human who was sinless
in nature as well as perfect in righteousness, He suffered
". . . outside the gate" (Heb. 13:12).

Christ's suffering leads us to another conclusion: *God
does not punish us when we ask "Why?"* Sometimes we forget
that when Jesus came face to face with suffering, He, too,
challenged God with the question, *"Why?"* In the Garden of
Gethsemane the anguish of the mind and the conflict of the
will so overwhelmed Him that He pleaded, "Father, if it is
possible, let this cup pass from Me" (Matt. 26:39). Within
that prayer are the questions, "Why me? Why this? Why
now?" Not many hours later when the sting of a thousand

scorpions took its toll, He cried out, "My God, why have You forsaken Me?"

Just recently a great and godly man died. When I asked his wife about his final days, she told me of the nightmare of his last twenty-four hours. No amount of drugs could dull the pain of a gentle man thrashing in the throes of death. Into the night she prayed for mercy, but toward the dawn her petition changed into protest against a God who seemed to have forsaken her. Who, including God, would blame her for asking, "Why?"

Hidden in the suffering of the sinless Jesus and the righteousness of Job is another thought that may escape us: *The closer we are to God, the greater can be our suffering.* By all means, we must avoid the idea that this is a formula for faith. Righteousness and suffering are no more a direct cause-and-effect relationship than are sin and suffering. Yet we know that each can be connected. The sinner who abuses the body may bring on suffering. Likewise a Christian in close communion with God may be as baffled as Jesus or Job when the suffering includes the silence of heaven. For him or her the question, "Why?" goes far deeper than the common protest of our humanity. With Jesus, his cry is, "My God, My God, why have You forsaken Me?" (Matt. 27:46).

Every truth about suffering can be twisted into a weapon for or against God. Only with hesitation do I draw one more conclusion. When amidst our suffering we ask "Why?", we also open ourselves to questions of "being right with God, doing right with things, and putting right for others." Generally speaking, suffering does not produce automatic reversals in character or conduct. Most often it speeds us in the direction we are already going—whether toward or away from God. Still, for those of us who believe God's enabling grace is at work with a love that is constantly nudging every person toward salvation, we must believe God can use suffering as one of those nudges. As Job learned from his friends, the danger comes when the nudge is turned into a sledgehammer.

We have not wandered very far from the central truth of Job's righteousness: *Suffering is no respecter of persons* and when we suffer, *God expects us to ask, "Why?"* Our comfort may be small but these truths are the beginning of faith.

3

How Satan Attacks

Never overestimate the power of Satan. In the deepest and darkest moments of our suffering, we are convinced that his power is unlimited and his control is complete. Job's story teaches us the opposite. Although Job feels betrayed by friends, forsaken by God, and assaulted by death, Satan's dominance is still frustrated by a shred of faith which Job will not let go. After reading the Book of Job, we know that Jesus does not exaggerate the truth to create an effect when He declares that faith the size of a mustard seed can move mountains. Furthermore, we know that Martin Luther writes inspired truth in the hymn, "A Mighty Fortress Is Our God"

> *. . . one little Word shall fell him.*

At the same time, we must never underestimate the power of Satan. He is a master strategist who employs every tactic to maximize the power under his control. Against Job, he utilizes every weapon in his arsenal. To know Satan's strategic and tactical weapons is to be better prepared to defend against them when our time of suffering comes.

The Strategy of Doubt

Critics of the Book of Job cannot explain how or why the drama of Job opens with Satan appearing among the sons of God in the council of heaven (Job 1:6). One answer is in the nature of God and His created beings. Even His angels are given the freedom of choice. According to scripture, the angel Lucifer plotted a *coup* against the authority of God which failed (Luke 10:18). Cast out of heaven with the one third of the angels who joined him, Lucifer and his rebellious corps became the restless spirits who roam the earth personifying evil and recruiting others into their ranks.

When God spots Satan among His sons in the council of heaven, He calls him out to ask where he has been and what he has been doing (Job 1:7). Perhaps God hopes that a lost son has come home. Instead, Satan reveals the tragedy of sin and alienation from God. He answers that he has been wandering to and fro over the earth. For those who wink at sin, this is a sober reminder of what it means to be lost—rootless, restless, aimless, and alone. Of course, this makes Satan doubly dangerous because he has nothing to do but exploit evil. As a paranoid person sees a threat in every cue of the environment, Satan sees the existence of evil in every form of physical nature and the potential for evil in every gift of human nature.

Peter's vivid picture of Satan as a roaring lion seeking whom he may devour is fair warning to us (1 Peter 5:8). An unguarded moment, a wayward eye, a moral flaw, a lingering doubt—at the slightest provocation, Satan strikes. While his tactics are as varied as the number of persons on the earth, his strategy is singular. Having learned his lesson when his rebellion in heaven failed, Satan always attacks the unguarded flank with a tempting question. As unbelievable as it may seem, he employs this strategy even in his confrontation with God at the meeting of heaven's council. In response to Satan's report on his wanderings, God asks him, "Have you considered My servant Job, that there is none like him on the earth, a blameless and upright man, one who fears God and shuns evil?" (Job 1:8).

Ever the cynic, Satan acknowledges that Job is a challenge to him, but he accuses God of giving His servant special protection and prosperity to assure his loyalty and obedience.

In Satan's snarling question, "Does Job serve You for nothing?" we see a re-run of the demonic strategy under which Adam fell and over which Jesus triumphed. Through Eve, Satan questioned God's integrity, authority, and power. When he inserted the doubt, "Did God really mean it when He said that you would die *if* you ate from the Tree of Life?" Adam took the bait and fell into sin.

With Jesus, Satan worked a variation on the same theme of challenging God's integrity, authority and wisdom.

> . . . *if* You are the Son of God, command that these stones become
> bread;
> . . . *if* You are the Son of God, throw yourself down;
> . . . *if* You will fall down and worship me (I will give You the
> kingdoms of the world) (Matt. 4:3, 6, 9).

"If" is the key word. A contingency is set up to introduce an element of doubt. Satan is a master at shifting the burden of proof to his victims. Jesus, however, refuses to take the bait. By citing the Word of God as the Truth, He puts the tempter back on the defensive without a comeback.

With us, Satan has not changed his strategy. He wanders over the earth in search of an opening into which he can insert a question that raises doubt about the integrity, authority, and wisdom of God. With Adam and Jesus, he used "If"; with us he uses, *"Why?"* Suffering is therefore a natural opening for Satan. When we ask "Why me? Why this? and Why now?" he utilizes every weapon in his arsenal to destroy our faith. If Satan has his way, we will curse God and die.

The Limits of His Power

God's give-and-take with Satan is like a two-sided coin. On one side is the image of Satan roaming the earth, exploiting doubt, preying on unwary souls, and even tempting God. On the other side is the image of God who is so secure He can

give His creation freedom of choice and so caring He draws
limits on the power of evil over our lives. When God permits
Satan to test Job's faith, He sets the terms, "Do not lay a hand
on his person." Job's fortune, fame, and family are put on the
line. As always, God's response can be read from the view of
skepticism or faith. Skepticism makes God a chess master
who manipulates Job in a game of pride. Faith sees the scene
through other eyes. God so trusts His servant Job that He
knows his faith will hold and grow under the test of suffering. He also knows Job's limits and will not permit Satan to
tempt him beyond what he can bear.

We stand in the presence of monumental truth. *God's
presence limits the power of Satan in our lives and in the world.*
For his family, fame, and fortune, Job acknowledges the protection and blessing of God with gratitude. Through his suffering, he learns that God lets Satan go just so far and no
farther.

Since studying the Book of Job, I see life differently. For
all God's gifts of grace in my life, I am more grateful because
I know they are evidences of His goodness, not my righteousness. For all the bad news which might lead us to think that
God has given up on His world, I know better. Evil may
appear to be having its day, but God sets the time and draws
the boundaries. For all who suffer, I know that God, not
Satan, sets limits for the power of evil. Death is the worst
Satan can do and for those with faith, "To live is Christ; to
die is gain" (Phil. 1:21). Whether in riches or poverty, sickness or health, calm or stress, comfort or persecution, it is
absolutely essential to remember that we live under the protection of God and are never abandoned by the presence of
God.

The Tactics of Evil

Although Satan's strategy is one-dimensional and his
power is limited, he employs so many varied and vicious tactics that he makes Machiavelli look like an amateur. None of
his weapons are of his own creation. He uses the effects of sin

in the physical order and in the human heart for his assaults.
Job's early calamities are an example. Satan strikes through
natural disaster and human depravity. Sabaens wipe out his
farms by rustling his oxen and asses; lightning causes a brush
fire which chars his sheep ranches; Chaldeans cut off his
caravan trade by stealing his camels; and a wild wind, most
likely a tornado, crushes all his children.

Accidents of nature are a conundrum to us. Insurance
companies define natural disasters as "acts of God." Their
theology is both right and wrong. Lightning bolts and torna-
does are within the natural order of God's creation and can
be explained by physical laws. Yet the weather remains essentially out of human control. While we tend to think of eco-
nomics as a science, experts confess the limits of their control
and the inexactitude of their craft. Each time I hear weather-
casters predict a 90 percent chance of rain I chuckle at their
cleverness and our gullibility. With such a prediction, they
cannot be wrong. If it rains, the 90 percent margin assures
the predictor's credibility. If it doesn't rain, the weather-
caster can still say, "It's within the 10 percent!" The truth is
that we can neither predict nor control the weather with 100
percent accuracy. Nature is full of surprises, some of which
cause horrendous human suffering.

At a little league baseball game one sultry evening, only
distant thunder signaled a brewing storm. Crackle and crash!
Without any other warning, a wildcat bolt of lightning struck
an eleven-year-old centerfielder and shocked the crowd into
ghastly silence. What are the chances that one bolt of lightning from a distant storm will strike an open baseball field
and sear an innocent boy standing in the outfield? The odds
are almost infinite and can be explained only as a random act
of nature, never as a deliberate act of God.

Whether Satan has some control over the acts of nature
which he exercises to bring calamity to Job is an open question. One thing is certain. He exploits the accidents of nature
to his own evil advantage. In Job's case, Satan either used or
exploited the accidents of nature to destroy the fortune and
family of a righteous man. If the Sabaens or Chaldeans had
slaughtered his children, Job would have had a target for his

rage. But Satan is too clever to give him that escape. By using a wild wind to crush his children, Satan enacts a slaughter without focus or blame. In such instances, the question "Why?" is aggravated—and God Himself becomes the target for protest against the evidence of His apparent injustice.

Satan has a more potent weapon in the evil intentions of the human heart. Whether calamity comes from the roving bands of Sabaen vandals or the calculated ambush of the Chaldeans, the motive is the same. In contrast with the accidents of nature which cause us to ask, "Why?" the suffering brought upon us by human evil causes us to add the question, "Who?" If we drive that question back to its source, we encounter the depravity of humanity and the evil intentions of men and women which Satan uses to work nefarious deeds, senseless atrocities, and unfathomable holocausts. At Dachau, whose name is synonymous with the Nazis' slaughter of the Jews in World War II, a black sign on a stone monument has been sculpted out of barbed wire letters which spell out the words, "Never Again." Our humanity makes that pledge after every holocaust, but the hard fact is that such events will not stop as long as our hearts are unredeemed and Satan exploits the evil in human nature.

Our church magazine carried the story of a father who picked up his five-year-old son for a weekend as part of a custody agreement in a divorce settlement. Promising the boy a trip to Disneyland, he took him to a motel and, while the child slept, poured kerosene over the bed, lit the fire, and drove away. Miraculously, the boy was rescued but not before he was burned over 90 percent of his body. Months of excruciating pain which the nurses described as "hell" left him totally disfigured and handicapped for life. Through the ordeal his mother has developed a calm and confident faith that includes forgiveness for the father. He, however, will soon be released from a short prison term with no apparent trace of remorse.

Whether the holocaust involves six million Jews or one five-year-old boy, we are constantly reminded that the unredeemed human heart is capable of evil beyond our imagination. Satan's power may be limited in the world, but we help him out. More often than not, his best weapon is to let us pursue our evil desires. He wins and others suffer.

The Point of Vulnerability

Contrary to Satan's claim, Job did not curse God and die when calamity wiped out his fortune and family. Rather, we see evidence that Job's relationship with God went far beyond the assurance of His protection and blessing. With gratitude, he received God's gifts but never took them for granted. Therefore, when they were taken away from him, Job gave us immortal words of faith which we now often repeat in the face of death. "The Lord gave, and the Lord has taken away; blessed be the name of the Lord" (1:21).

So Satan failed in his first attack. But persistence is another of his weapons. Reappearing among the Sons of God in the council of heaven, Satan is chided by God: "Have you considered My servant Job, that there is none like him on the earth, a blameless and upright man, one who fears God and shuns evil? And still he holds fast to his integrity, although you incited Me against him, to destroy him without cause" (Job 2:3).

In response, Satan spits through his teeth the oath, "Skin for skin," and declares that he failed only because God still protected Job from personal attack. With full trust in His servant, God lifts His hand of protection from the person of Job but forces Satan to stop short of death itself.

Satan has revealed his ultimate weapon. In attacking us, he probes and probes until he finds our *point of vulnerability*. His assumption is that each of us has a price for which we will deny our faith, curse God, and die. In Job's case, Satan made the error of thinking that the man's circle of faith did not go beyond his fortune and his family. For many of us, Satan's assumption might have been true. If we faced the sudden loss of all the blessings of God which we take for granted, would we remain faithful? Few of us have ever been put to that test. Perhaps God knows our limits and protects us from the attacks of Satan. If so, the absence of this test may be an indictment upon the smallness of our trust and the shallowness of our relationship with God. Faith grows large and deep only when it is tested.

Job's priorities are revealed by Satan's earlier probes. In succession calamity wipes out his farms, ranches, caravans, and children. In the economy of the East, we can presume that Job's greatness escalated as he expanded his empire from local farms and vast ranches to the international trade routes plied by camel caravans. Although the Book of Job does not specify the time interval between calamities, Job had sufficient time to react to the tragic news brought by each of the messengers who survived disaster. If he had cursed God at any point, Satan would have discontinued his attacks. Instead, Satan struck and struck again until he came as close to Job as he could without afflicting his person. The order of Satan's attacks tells us much about Job's priorities. Professionally, he loved his reputation as an international trader whose camel caravans plied the trade routes of the East. But business took second place to his love for his family, especially his children.

When I first read Job's story, I reacted against the apparent ease with which he responded to the loss of his children as well as his possessions by saying, "The Lord gave, and the Lord has taken away; Blessed be the name of the Lord." Still later, however, we learn the depth of hurt which Job suffered when he lost his children. His three friends, Eliphaz, Bildad, and Zophar, each took a turn at trying to connect some unknown sin in Job's life with the death of his children. But later on, as Job recalled the time when God blessed him, he did not count oxen, asses, sheep, or camels (Job 29). Rather, he remembered the moments together with his children and he anticipated old age as a father and grandfather who would see many generations of his family. To lump the death of his children in with the loss of his material possessions is to misread Job. When the tempter crushed Job's beloved sons and daughters in the tornado, Satan struck as close to the heart of Job as he could without attacking the man himself.

Satan has not changed his tactics. He still persists in probing and probing until he finds our point of vulnerability. He still assumes that our motives are basically selfish, whether for our possessions, our children, or ourselves. Therefore, even though he fails to break Job's faith by his early onslaughts, he blames God for protecting his point of vulnerability, namely his body and his ego. By afflicting him with a physically painful, psychologically depressing, and socially detestable disease, Satan concludes that he will find the fatal flaw in the blameless and upright character of Job.

Another attestation to the righteousness of Job is the fact that Satan can attack him only from the outside. No evil desire or hidden lust gives Satan a beachhead within Job from which to launch his attack. He must resort to the effect of sin in the natural order. In this case, Satan uses either Job's hereditary weakness or environmental influence to cause the most grotesque of physical diseases.

Within ourselves each of us has a susceptibility to a variety of physical diseases. As long as we are healthy, the diseases are kept dormant by the defense systems of the body. If, however, our defense systems are broken down, we become vulnerable to diseases peculiar to us due to hereditary or environmental influences. Diabetes, for instance, is heavily affected by hereditary factors. Skin cancer, however, is on the rise due to sunbathing in polluted air penetrated by ultraviolet rays. Hereditary factors, such as skin pigment, are still not ruled out. A fair-skinned person who disregards the doctor's cautions about exposure to the sun is inviting the kind of cancer for which he or she has a weakness.

Satan also knows our psychological point of vulnerability. Each of us has a different tolerance level for tension. Persons with a high threshold can cope with multiple stress factors. Those with a low threshold of stress, however, may buckle under the weight of a single factor. Holmes' scale of stress, for instance, identifies 100 stress experiences in descending order.[1] At the top are such factors as divorce, death of a spouse, change of position, and moving to a new location. The most stressful situation is to combine several of these high stress factors into a cluster of stresses within a short time frame. Everyone will show some signs of trauma during such times, but depending upon the threshold of stress, one person might break under the strain while another might gain strength. It all depends upon our vulnerability to stress.

One of the arguments criminologists use against capital punishment for murder is the difference between an "habitual killer" and an "episodic murderer." An "habitual killer" is a hardened criminal who murders by vicious design. An "episodic murderer" is a person who is caught in a collapsing web of circumstances that causes an unusual and temporary reaction of violence. Presumably, a person could be caught in such a web of circumstances which provoke murder only once in a lifetime and therefore should be rehabilitated rather than executed. A related assumption is that every person has the potential for violence given the right set of circumstances. In other words, in the social as well as the psychological and physical setting, each of us has his or her point of vulnerability. The contest is ever on. As long as we live, Satan will persistently probe for our weaknesses with the demonic hope of finding our "fatal flaw."

While Satan's goal is to make us suffer, the story of Job teaches us that the devil's power is limited by the protection of God and frustrated by His presence. Satan's strategy is singular. He tries to get us to turn the question "Why?" into doubt about God's integrity, authority, and wisdom. His tactics, however, are multiple. Using the effects of sin in the physical order and human nature, Satan is a terrorist who customizes his attacks to fit the circumstances and takes his victims by surprise. Especially through accidents of the physical order and the leanings of the human heart, he probes until he finds our point of vulnerability. Here is where we truly suffer; here is where our faith is fully tested. Under Satan's attack through suffering, we will either curse God and die or trust God and grow.

"Why did I not die at birth?"
—Job

4
How Suffering Hurts

Suffering speaks with an eloquence all its own. After
Satan launches his attack upon the person of Job, the good
and great man is reduced to a living corpse. His disease is so
devastating that his wife urges him to curse God and die; city
officials consign him to an ashheap outside the protective
gates; and his closest friends give him up for dead. With one
last toss of ashes over their heads, they turn and walk away.
Knowing the sign of death, Job musters enough strength to
raise his head and shout after them, "Why did I not die at
birth?" (Job 3:11).

Job is hurt far beyond his physical pain. When we
suffer, we hurt all over. Our suffering is physical, mental,
social, and spiritual. The totality of our hurt can be heard in
the initial questions of suffering, "Why me? Why this? Why
now?" The wholeness of our hurt can be felt in the attacks
of Satan—sometimes against our body, often against our
minds, usually against our pride, and always against our
faith.

The Wholeness of Suffering

The wholeness of suffering sounds like a contradiction. In medicine, "wholeness" is health; in psychology, it is maturity; in religion, it is holiness. Ideally, all this is true. Practically, we must admit that we treat the body, mind, and spirit as separate entities with limited interaction. Specialists in medicine, psychology, and theology, for instance, seldom talk together about the problems of persons they label patients, clients, or parishioners. As ironic as it may seem, the link between the mind and body in physical illness was formally introduced only forty or so years ago as "psychosomatic medicine." Even more ironically, doctors in this field found themselves suspended in limbo between medicine and psychology. A specialist in psychosomatic medicine did not fit the professional definition of either a physician or a psychologist. The issue is still not fully resolved.

Today, the connection between the spiritual aspect of personality and psychophysical health is another new frontier. Researchers are exploring the spiritual dimensions of physical and emotional health with positive results. In practice, some pioneers are venturing into the field of "holistic medicine," but not without some negative reaction from specialists in medicine, psychology, and religion. Attitudes toward the professionals in this developing field range from "wait-and-see" skepticism to outright charges of quackery.

While specialists squabble over definitions, the Bible leaves no doubt about the unity of body, mind, and spirit. Whether it is God's creative work or the redemptive mission of Christ, our physical, emotional, and spiritual being is one. When Christ makes us whole, He heals our bodies, renews our minds, and redeems our souls. Just this morning in the foyer of a church I met a man whom I hardly recognized. Each of us was thousands of miles from home and out of our familiar context. More than that, he was a trim figure with a bright look in his eyes. The man I had known weighed fifty pounds more and smiled only out of professional courtesy. A second look, however, told me that I was wrong. The trim and smiling fellow visitor was one and the same person. After we had greeted each other, I paid him the compliment, "You look absolutely great! How did you do it?" He then told me his doctor had given him the ultimatum to lose weight or face the consequences of high blood pressure. In the oft-repeated words of people for whom weight loss has restored their self-esteem, he beamed, "I had forgotten what it means to feel good about myself." In that sentence, he spoke a truth we easily forget. In health, maturity, and holiness, our bodies, minds, and spirits are one.

While we are still struggling with the unity of body, mind, and spirit in health, we may resist the idea of wholeness in suffering. Logic counters our resistance. If we are one in body, mind, and spirit, we are one in suffering and in health. Furthermore, we know that the effect of sin is total. No part of our person is outside its depravity. Therefore, if we can be made whole in health, we are also susceptible to wholeness in suffering. For those who suffer, such truth is experiential as well as logical. In suffering all systems of body, mind, and spirit interact. Physical pain makes it difficult to think or pray; emotional stress causes physical breakdown and spiritual despair; and alienation from God compounds physical ills and magnifies mental distress. The whole of suffering, then, is greater than the pain of its parts.

Job is our prime example. For those of us who remember him only as a man covered with boils, a deeper look into his experience shows us a person driven to the brink of blasphemy and the edge of self-destruction by the wholeness of suffering.

The Dimensions of Suffering

Satan chose physical disease as his point of entry into the personality of Job. A rather simple diagnosis informs us that boils covered him from head to foot (Job 2:7). For a person who remembers having one boil as a teenager, I cringe at the thought of having my skin turned into one swollen, oozing mass of boils coming to a head. Medically, boils might be fatal. But even the thought of the excruciating pain and the distortion of face and figure is enough to make one wish for death. It is doubtful, however, that boils were diagnosed as a contagious disease which required quarantine on an ashheap outside the city with the expectation of imminent death. Other physical symptoms which we discover in Job's case are clues to a more dreadful and disfiguring disease. Job's medical chart also shows:

. . . itching, open sores (2:7–8)
. . . insomnia (7:4)
. . . cracking and blistering of the skin (7:5)
. . . maggots bred in ulcers (7:5)
. . . total exhaustion (16:7)
. . . putrid breath (19:17)
. . . rotting teeth (19:20)
. . . loss of weight (19:20)
. . . weakening of bones (30:17)
. . . diarrhea (30:27)
. . . blackening of the skin (30:30)
. . . high fever (30:30)

Two other diagnostic possibilities need to be considered from this syndrome of symptoms. One is *elephantiasis:* a rare disease characterized by gross and distorted enlargement of body extremities along with the blackening and blistering of the skin. For those who remember the provocative, prize-winning film, "Elephant Man," we can understand why Job appeared to face early death in the crude isolation ward of an ashheap. If elephantiasis is a disease that modern medicine still cannot cure and modern society cannot accept, certainly we can sympathize with the dilemmas of ancient medicine and society in Job's day. To understand Job's suffering, we must think of him as the leper of Jesus' day or the AIDS victim of our day.

An alternative diagnosis is a disease peculiar to Job's time and region. It may be called the *"3-D Disease"* because its symptoms are dermatitis, diarrhea, and dementia. Blackened, leathered, blistered, and cracked skin is symptomatic of dermatitis. Job's embarrassed complaint about his uncontrolled bowels leaves no doubt about diarrhea. All this combined with hallucinations, the sad sign of dementia in the mind of a man who had once been a leader of thought in the Wisdom School of the East.

Whatever the disease with which Satan plagued Job, the symptoms tell us something about his point of vulnerability. As the greatest man in the East, Job may well have been a person with a face and physique complementing his wealth and power so that his presence dominated any setting. A presidential reception at the White House comes to mind. Leaders who are movers and shakers in their own right cluster in cliques waiting for the host to appear. Then there is a hush. The door opens and the President of the United States walks in. He looks taller than expected and bears an aura of dignity that is unmatched in the room. No flaws of face or figure are tolerated. Image is essential to his position, power, and presence.

Job must have brought this same kind of image to any setting in which he appeared. In his reflections of the days of his glory, he remembers that young men hid from him, old men stood in his honor, princes stopped talking, and nobles became tongue-tied in his presence (Job 29:8–10). Imagine, then, Job's face twisted and his physique emaciated by the ravages of disease. Who can blame him as he pleaded for the relief of death even though he knew it meant personal obliteration in the land of shadows without the hope of eternal life in the presence of God? Satan's attack upon Job's appearance may have brought him close to his point of vulnerability.

Even though the pain of Job's physical disease pushed him to the edge of death, his psychological suffering hurt even more. Closely connected with the pain of his bodily illness are the horrors of his dementia:

> . . . a wish to die (3:11)
> . . . a haunting fear (3:25)
> . . . no taste for life (6:6)
> . . . utter futility (7:8–9)
> . . . terror by night (7:14)
> . . . delusions by day (7:14)
> . . . depression (7:16)
> . . . bitter anger (10:59)

. . . a broken spirit (17:1)
. . . hallucinations (30:15)

Only one who has been through such emotional suffering can fully empathize with Job's plight. Anton Boisen wrote
an unforgettable book entitled *The Exploration of the Inner
World*. It is an autobiographical account of Boisen's torturous
journey from mental health to a severe form of psychosis
which required institutionalization. Like a psychological
Lazarus, Boisen came back from emotional death to tell
about his experience. Because of that he could write:

> To be plunged as a patient into a hospital for the insane may be a
> tragedy or it may be an opportunity. For me it has been an opportu-
> nity. It has introduced me to a new world of absorbing interest and
> profound significance; it has shown me that world throughout its
> entire range, from the bottommost depths of the nether regions to
> the heights of religious experience at its best; it has made me aware
> of certain relationships between two important fields of human
> experience, which thus far have been held strictly apart; and has
> given me a task in which I find the meaning and purpose of my life.[1]

The pain of a tortured mind is often worse than death.
As a hospital chaplain, I ministered to many patients whose
fatal disease caused pain not even drugs could dull. A
Methodist minister, for instance, came to my ward for treat-
ment of lung cancer in its advanced stage. His gentle spirit,
ready smile, and pastoral prayers transformed the gloomy
ward into a sanctuary for the presence of God. He ministered to me. But within days his pain became so acute that
surgeons performed a prefrontal lobotomy to alter the intolerable sense of pain. After the brain surgery, his personality
underwent a complete change—raging anger, vulgar language, and brute strength. Still the pain persisted. When I
visited him for the last time, I prayed for the mercy of a quick
death while he swore at me. Within hours, God answered my
prayer.

My internship in a mental hospital left me with another
impression of suffering—the sights and sounds of tormented
minds. Half-naked bodies, people clawing at walls, curled
into permanent fetal positions, or a person spending twenty
hours a day pounding an imaginary typewriter with a click of

fingers to sound the bell for the carriage return—these scenes will never leave me. Most of these people are still there suffering in their own private hell year after year. There is a pain worse than death.

Most of us know only fleeting moments of extreme emotional suffering. What would it be like to go night after night into terror-filled dreams which awaken you dripping with sweat and shaking with chills? Just the other night, our son dreamed of an airliner smashing into a skyscraper and killing all the passengers. The nightmare was so real that he awakened with the compulsion to call across country and tell us to take a different flight from a western city the next day.

What would it be like to prolong the anxiety that grinds up our stomachs in tension-filled times for a lifetime? Or to make a permanent mental state out of those occasions when life is as flat and tasteless as the white of an egg? Or when our self-worth is like a cipher with the rim knocked off? Or when the thought of tomorrow seems as futile as rearranging the deck chairs on the *Titanic?* All these emotions, from the extremes of borderline psychosis to the extension of crippling anxiety, crashed at once on the psyche of Job. He knew the experience of emotional suffering that is far worse than death.

Relational Suffering

Job's psychological suffering extended to his interpersonal relationships. We first met him as an immensely attractive social creature and as a family man who loved a celebration. Consequently, his disgraceful disease caused another extreme form of suffering—estrangement from those whom he loved and on whom he counted. Attention is usually focused upon his wife who urged him to curse God and die rather than fight intolerable pain. Because of her urging, she is often condemned as the devil's handmaiden. More generously, Job's wife is cited for her lack of faith. Job preferred to call her "foolish," which charges her only with the inability to see the larger picture through eyes of faith. The lesson applies to all who suffer. If we lose sight of the big picture which can only be seen through the eyes of faith, we give up and die. Faith is essentially a viewpoint with the big picture in mind. Is this not what the apostle Paul means when he writes that our suffering, whatever it may be, is always temporary?

Job's wife has my sympathy. In fact, her urging for Job to curse God and die may be proof of her love for her husband which Satan turned into his own tool. Until we have stood at the bedside and prayed for God to take the life of a family member experiencing insufferable pain from a terminal illness, we should be slow to condemn Job's wife. In her love for her husband, Satan found the point of her vulnerability. As any husband or wife, father or mother knows, it is easier to suffer ourselves than it is to stand by helplessly while those whom we love writhe in anguish.

Assuming that Job's wife and children occupied the center of his network of human relationships, we see that network break down from the inside out until Job is totally alone, without any kind of human support. After his children are dead and his wife urges him to curse God and die, we learn later that all his brothers, sisters, and acquaintances withdraw from him as well (Job 42:11). According to his own words, Job is faced with the disgrace of being taunted by young men whose fathers Job would not even trust with the dogs of his flocks (Job 30:1). The rabble spits upon him and use his name as a byword (Job 30:9). His social rejection is almost complete. Not only is he isolated from the community, but he is ostracized by the lowest of its people.

Job still has his three closest friends who come to comfort him—Eliphaz, Bildad, and Zophar. In the long run, they turn out to be the kind of friends that no suffering person needs. But not enough can be said about the quality of their friendship with Job that brought them from distant cities to the side of their friend. According to the Scriptures, Eliphaz, Bildad, and Zophar lived in three separate cities (Job 2:11). When the news of Job's plight reached them, they corresponded with each other and agreed to meet at a common point from which they would travel to Job's home. At the first sight of Job on the ashheap, they did not recognize him (Job 3:12). A closer look convinced them that his death was imminent. Without a word, they went into the rite of mourning, shredding their robes and throwing ashes into the air. The depth of their friendship is indicated by their presence, their grief, and their silence. They and they alone stayed with Job in his disgrace (Job 2:13).

Even their friendship had limits, however. After they fulfilled their obligation for seven days of mourning, the three friends walked away and left their friend for dead. They forgot a fundamental fact about persons who are on the edge of death. Their sensitivities are sharpened by pain and their reactions are aggravated. So, when Job saw his last human support walking away, he cried out after them,

> Why did I not die at birth?
> Why did I not perish when I came
>   from the womb?
> (Job 3:11)
>
> Why?. . . Why? . . . Why?
> (Job 3:12–23)

His friends repudiated Job's cry because they heard it as an attack on the integrity of God. They failed to hear his cry for help. Because they missed the meaning of his cry, Job likened them to streams in the desert upon which weary caravan travelers depend to quench their thirst. To come to the streams and find them dry is to dash the hopes of the travelers. Like the dry streams, Job says, "My brothers have dealt deceitfully" (Job 6:15).

Spiritual Suffering

Abandonment by family and betrayal by friends border on the most severe suffering we can know. Still, a person can survive suffering without a human network if he or she feels there is a spiritual connection with God and God's people. Physical pain, emotional despair, and relational loss would seem to be enough to make a person give up. But as long as spiritual supports remain, people of faith can still be strong in suffering. A common testimony is for a person who has come through suffering to say, "Except for the prayers of

God's people, I would not have made it." Anyone who is a
member of a Christian congregation knows what it means to
be lifted by love and help from brothers and sisters in Christ.

The man whose home burned to the ground told me
that he and his wife were still in transition between churches
when the tragedy occurred. They thought that all the real
love remained in the congregation from which they had to
move in a career change. But when fire left them homeless,
they found out that Christian love is not confined to a given
location. They wept in gratitude as their new church friends
opened their homes, gave them clothes, and even furnished
their new home.

Job's experience is just the opposite. In one of the sad-
dest notes of scripture, he remembers standing up in the
congregation of the righteous and crying out for help (Job
30:28). He might as well have shouted to the barren desert.
At least, he would have heard the echo of his own voice.
Instead, the pain of silence from the congregation is spoken
in the heartrending words,

> I am a brother of jackals,
> And a companion of ostriches.
> (Job 30:29)

On this mournful note, we are informed that every last
web in Job's network of human relationships has broken
down (19:13–20). Still, as a man of faith, his despair is not
complete. Job has a lifetime of communion and friendship
with God who confirms that relationship in His commendation to Satan, "Have you considered My servant Job, that
there is none like him on the earth, a blameless and upright
man, one who fears God and shuns evil?" (Job 1:8).

To understand the wholeness of Job's suffering, we must
realize that Job does not break communion or fellowship
with God. His suffering, however, leads him to believe that
God has abandoned him (23:8–9), refuses to answer him
(9:16), and even attacks him like a vicious animal which tears
at his flesh and shakes him in his teeth (Job 16:9–12).

Every honest person who suffers will admit to moments
of doubt when he or she feels abandoned by God and moments of despair when it seems as if God has become a vicious

adversary. In those moments, we are teetering on the edge of hopelessness. If Satan can convince us that we have been abandoned by God, life will lose its meaning. Short of death itself, that is Satan's vicious aim for our suffering. If he can use suffering to destroy the meaning of life, he has created the despair that causes us to curse God and die.

In his book *The Sickness Unto Death* Kierkegaard uses a fable to describe the spiritual suffering of despair.[2] A knight is pursuing a rare bird with the hope of catching it. But each time he feels sure of seizing it, the bird flies just beyond his reach. The frustrating quest goes on until darkness falls and the knight suddenly realizes he has lost his way and does not know where he is. In Job's most bitter cry against God, we hear the same loss of hope:

> Leave me alone,
> That I may take a little comfort,
> Before I go to the place from which
> I shall not return,
> To the land of darkness
> and the shadow of death, . . .
> *Where* even the light is like darkness.
> (Job 10:20–22)

Remember that Job lived in a time before the reality of heaven had been revealed. Therefore, his spiritual suffering went even deeper than ours. Without the promise of life after death, his only hope depended upon staying alive.

The Ultimate Suffering

In the wholeness of Job's physical, mental, relational, and spiritual suffering, we catch a glimpse of the suffering of Jesus Christ. Described by Isaiah as "the Suffering Servant," Jesus experienced a thousand scorpions' teeth in physical pain, mind-breaking mental anguish, back-stabbing betrayal, the social disgrace of a criminal's death, and the abandonment of His Father. Like Job, Jesus suffered wholly; like Job, Jesus struggled to retain hope against mounting despair. Unlike Job, however, Jesus' suffering was ultimate as well as whole. He and He alone knows the finality of physical

death, psychological despair, social disgrace, personal betrayal, and spiritual abandonment. Yet, in His suffering is our
hope. To paraphrase the well-known promise, "There is no
suffering known to man which He has not experienced."

For all who suffer or minister to those who suffer, the
story of Job reminds us that our pain does not come in pieces.
While at one time or another the focus of our pain may be
magnified, because we are created as beings of interlocking
mind, body, and spirit, our suffering is whole. Like ripples on
a pond, wherever the pebble of suffering strikes us, the
waves of pain roll through our total personality and wash
over our whole being. When we are engulfed by suffering,
the temptation is to give up hope, lose the meaning of life,
curse God, and die. If we do, Satan trumpets his triumph.

No matter how complete our suffering or how deep our
despair, we must not forget that Jesus went through and
beyond our suffering for us. He and He alone experienced
ultimate and total suffering. Because of Him, however, we
have this assurance: we suffer nothing that He has not
known. Far more than that, Jesus met the ultimate attack of
Satan in death and rose triumphant. Thus, our response to
suffering is more than "toughing it out." Tough we must be,
but triumphant we *will* be. As Jesus holds the keys to death
and hell, He also holds the keys to our suffering. In health or
sickness, life or death, we have His assurance, "My grace is
sufficient for you."

5
How Friends Fail

Suffering is a test of friendship. Compassion wells up within us the moment we hear of calamity striking a friend. Immediately, we respond with a telephone call, a sympathy card, a prayer, and a visit. Then what happens? We go back to our business and tend to forget friends who suffer until a guilty recollection prompts us to repeat our show of sympathy with another card, call, prayer, and visit.

Although I forget more often than I remember, I have discovered an open door for ministry by sending a card or a note to people several weeks after they have suffered the loss of a loved one. In the days immediately following death, grief is cushioned by shock—but when the shock wears off and reality returns, lonely nights and despairing days take over. As a widow of six months said recently, "My husband used to do the grocery shopping with me. Now every time I go to the grocery store, I break down in tears."

The real test of suffering on friendship is long-term. Quick compassion is commendable, but long-term love is what suffering people need. Even now, an image haunts my mind. Four or five times a year, my wife and I make an

800-mile round trip to visit her mother, one of God's choic-
est servants. In her nineties and senile, she is a permanent
resident of a nursing home. Each time we walk through the
front door of the home, we are greeted by a welcoming
committee of aged people who sit in the lobby waiting for
someone to come and visit them. Their searching eyes speak
volumes as they scan our faces to see if we are family or
friends. Seeing no familiar faces, they only grunt when we
say "hello" and look past us through the front door once
again.

Job's three friends deserve our highest commendation
for their genuine compassion when they hear of the calamity
that has befallen him. How many friends do we have who
would take the time and spend the money to come from
distant cities and travel together through a wild and treach-
erous land to visit us in our suffering (Job 2:11)? A note or a
gift might have been sufficient.

There is a time when we must go personally to family
and friends who are suffering. A colleague's brother con-
tracted AIDS and confessed a hidden history of gay encoun-
ters. Despite the dread and the disgrace of the disease, our
friend said, "He's my brother. I must go to him." No one
questioned his decision. Even then, his love took a jolt when
he first glimpsed the wasted body of his diseased brother and
realized that his love was destined for a long-term test.

The love of Job's friends also was jolted when they first
saw him. While still at a distance, they squinted through the
desert sun at a bundle of blackened skin and bones on an
ashheap outside the city gates (Job 2:12). They could not
handle the sight. Ripping off their clothes and throwing
ashes into the air, they fell into mournful silence for seven
days (Job 2:13). Just because we know the rest of the story,
we must not write off Job's friends too quickly. In the beginning, Eliphaz, Bildad, and Zophar were the kind of friends
we need when we suffer. They put everything aside to visit
their friend, showed shock at the sight of him, and stayed by
his side in silence after his family and other friends had abandoned him. As with most of us who confront suffering, they
failed by giving up too soon.

Giving Up Too Soon

As long as we hold a shred of hope, we can stand suffering. Job's friends gave him that hope during the seven days when they sat with him in silence. As we noted earlier, abandonment is the cause of despair and with it goes the meaning of life. Viktor Frankl, the psychiatrist, developed his logotherapy out of his experience in a Nazi extermination camp. He noted a difference between the prisoners who survived and those who succumbed to brutality. Survivors were those people who had something to live for—whether faith, family, or future. Those whose lives had lost their meaning, however, died without the will to fight.

We cannot place enough value on the assuring presence of family and friends during the time of suffering. Nothing need be said. In fact, it is usually the anxiety of the visitor that forces an awkward conversation. "How are you?" is one of the most ridiculous questions we can ask. The suffering person must either lie to please us or be honest and provoke us to recite platitudes of reassurance. To the credit of Job's friends, they let their presence speak for them. The value of those moments is later reflected in Job's pitiful prayer when they are in the heat of debate:

> Oh, that you would be silent
> And it would be your wisdom!
> (Job 13:5)

There is good reason for the silent presence of family and friends during the time of suffering. When a person is in pain, whether physical, psychological, social, or spiritual, the atmosphere is heavily charged with sensitivity to the cues that betray our unspoken feelings. As a former hospital chaplain, I remember the *faux pas* of a ministerial student who read the Psalm, "The Lord will not suffer thy foot to be moved." His patient was a man whose right foot had just been amputated! I also remember a family who had just been informed that their father had a fatal disease. When they entered his room, they tried to hide their feelings by engaging in bad jokes and nervous chatter. The father instantly perceived their awkwardness and stopped them in mid-laughter with the question, "It's over, isn't it?"

We forget that the suffering person has all five senses sharpened to a razor's edge, along with an intuitive sixth sense. Again, in the hospital chaplaincy, we were warned that a muffled whisper across the room may be heard as a shout by a dying person. Or that the lowering of the eyes in answer to a patient's question can expose a visual answer that we cannot dodge with the most nimble of verbal sidesteps.

Job's friends lack these insights. After seven days, they give him up for dead and walk away. Little do they realize that their presence gave Job hope. Even less do they realize what their leaving means to him. When they walk away, Job sees something through fevered eyes that drives him to a violent verbal reaction. Hysterically, he screams after them:

> Why did I not die at birth?
> (Job 3:11)

> For the thing I greatly feared
> has come upon me,
> And what I dreaded
> has happened to me.
> (Job 3:25)

The sight of his friends walking away triggers the fear of abandonment that each of us feels deep within his being. Job faces what we fear. As close as Job might have been to God, he still needed the assurance of a human face. With the loss of his friends, Job not only feels abandoned but will test a relationship between himself and his unseen God without the benefit of human support.

Failing to Listen

By his own admission, Job's cry is angry, rash, and bitter. How else can we cry *Why?* from the brink of death and despair? If our cry is genuine, it cannot sound like a mere academic question raised in a neutral setting. Many interpreters of the Book of Job fail at this point. They sterilize the setting and intellectualize the "Why?" Put yourself in Job's place. His suffering is total, his death is imminent, his righteousness is intact, and his last three friends have given him up for dead. Who wouldn't cry, "May the day I was born be cursed"?

From the innermost recesses of his being, Job vents the bitterness which suffering people feel, but are usually afraid to express. Perhaps our guilt holds us back. If so, we understand why Job does not hesitate to vent his feelings. He is a righteous man for whom guilt is no barrier. His cry comes right from his spleen, the source of the body's most bitter bile.

Job's friends couldn't handle such an outburst. They heard his words, but do not listen to the meaning of his cry. To them, Job violates every rule of moderation that characterizes the wise man. In Job's rash words, Eliphaz, Bildad, and Zophar hear only the raving of a fool and the rebellion of a blasphemer (Job 15:2–6). If only they had listened to the meaning of Job's cry, they would have heard a desperate appeal for help from friends in whom he still had confidence. They were his court of last resort in the human context. But instead of hearing his appeal, they stumble on protocol and condemn their friend. Because they refuse to listen to the meaning of Job's cry, they provoke a dialogue of escalating rage and deteriorating substance that ends in a silent, sullen stalemate.

During the campus revolt of the early 1970s, a student leader spewed venom against me as president of a university. Years earlier, I had learned never to respond to a personal attack in public, so I invited her into my office. Knowing her parents and caring for her, I asked her why she had resorted to such tactics. Her answer surprised me when she said, "Don't you know when you hear a cry for help?" Since then, I have tried to listen for the meaning of people's words, especially when they are hostile. So often, the sound and the meaning are not the same.

Job's dialogue with his three friends illustrates the consequences of failure to listen. After Job cries out in anguish, the dialogue falls into this deteriorating pattern:

Eliphaz: "You have sinned" (4:17).
Job: "You are no help" (6:21).

Bildad: "You are full of hot air" (8:2).
   Job: "God is my adversary" (10:16).
Zophar: "You mock God" (11:3).
   Job: "You mock me" (12:4).
Eliphaz: "You are a fool" (15:2).
   Job: "You are miserable comforters" (16:2).
Bildad: "You shut up" (18:2).
   Job: "You crush me" (19:2).
Zophar: "You insult us" (20:3).
   Job: "You listen just once" (21:2).
Eliphaz: "You are wicked" (22:2–3).
   Job: "I will trust God" (23:10).
Bildad: "You are a maggot" (25:6)!
   (End of conversation.)

The heated debate ends with a demeaning and dehumanizing insult. Silence follows. Close friends who once loved each other have nothing more to say. Eliphaz, Bildad, and Zophar came to comfort Job. Instead, they aggravated his suffering and added to his grief. To them, a beloved friend became a groveling worm. If only they had listened!

Spiritualizing Too Easily

Job's friends also failed him when they glibly spiritualized his suffering. Spiritualizing comes in many forms and has two extremes. One extreme is a Pollyanna attitude. The most common form of a spiritualized Pollyanna response is to quote the Scripture to a suffering soul, "For we know that all things work together for them who love the Lord." Try telling that to Job on an ashheap!

During my college days, a student friend worked in a local woodworking shop to pay her school bills. In an unguarded moment, she placed her hand on a running table saw and severed it at the wrist. After coming out of surgery, she was "comforted" by her employer with this spiritual Pollyannism, "Thank God it was only a hand. You might have lost an arm." Try telling that to Job on an ashheap.

Evidently Job's friends tried a bit of spiritual Pollyanna

on him. At least at the beginning of their exchange, they balanced out their indictment of his sin with poetic promises of restored health, prosperity, and peace. In a biting response, Job reminds them:

> I also could speak as you do,
> If your soul were in my soul's place.
> (Job 16:4)

While Job's sarcasm is primarily intended to refute their "windy words" and "miserable comfort," he is referring to their easy spiritualizing as well.

The other extreme of spiritualizing is worse than the Pollyanna panacea. When Job splits the air with his anguished cry, "Why was I born?" his three friends interpret it as an attack on God rather than a cry for help. Of necessity, then, they take it upon themselves to defend God—the most arrogant of human assumptions. Fanaticism is the result. A fanatic is appropriately defined as a person who acts as God would act . . . if God had all the facts. Or a fanatic approaches issues with the attitude of a young boy who purported to draw a picture of God. When informed by an adult that no one knew what God looked like, the confident artist answered, "When I'm through, they will."

Job's friends speak as if they have all the facts and know God's thoughts ahead of Him. So, they jump to judgment and diagnose Job's distress the result of sin. The truth of the matter is that Job's outburst is a personal threat to their security and authority. Suffering people often do shocking things. One of the gentlest spirits I have known thrashed and raged in the final hours before death. His wife reported that the nightmare of those hours will never leave her because she did not know how to handle the shock of his reaction. In similar fashion, Job's angry and bitter call after his departing friends terrifies them. Job, whom they had known as a thoughtful man who modeled the moderation of wisdom, exploded in a rage that they could not handle. Job himself said to them, "You see terror and are afraid" (Job 6:21).

Suffering determines whether or not we can accept a violent and unexpected reaction from a friend, particularly when it might be interpreted as a personal attack. In his book

Dialogue of Despair, William Hulme draws the difference between responding and reacting to the expression of a friend's
frustration. If, he says, the needs of the other person are the
center of our attention, we respond by accepting his outburst
as an expression of these needs. If, however, the focus is upon
our own needs, we will be threatened by the needs of others
and react defensively against them.[1] Friendship that serves
only to bolster our own needs will break down under such a
test.

   More than their security is at stake. Job's violent reaction is a threat to the authority of his three friends. Eliphaz,
for instance, is the eldest and presumably the wisest of the
three friends. His first response to Job is spoken in the tone
of a benevolent father. Yet, by appealing to a special nighttime vision as the source of his authority, Eliphaz declares
that sin is the root cause of Job's suffering. When Job disputes
Eliphaz's authority as an elder and contends for his innocence, Job is defending the essence of his self-esteem. Bildad
labels him a "bag of wind" (8:2), and Zophar indicts him for
mocking authority (11:3).

   When our egos are threatened, we seldom choose a direct counterattack. No one really wants to admit to a tender
ego. So we find a more acceptable base from which to launch
our counterattack. Religious people, in particular, may
choose to spiritualize the issue to gain a formidable weapon.
Eliphaz, Bildad, and Zophar choose this tactic for their counterattack on Job. By posing as the defenders of the faith
against a person whom they progressively label as sinful, rebellious, and wicked, they presume to be on God's side.

   On my desk at this moment is a letter of criticism which
begins, "Before writing to you, I sought the mind of
God . . . ." The writer then goes on to make caustic judgments against a person whom he does not know and draws
damning conclusions without the facts. Neither love nor reason prevails.

   Under the same guise, Zophar attacks Job. Presuming
to speak for God, he goes beyond Eliphaz and Bildad's accusation of sin to denounce him as a "wicked man" who is perva-
sively evil (20:29). What defense does Job have? He chooses
the only alternative open to him—a direct appeal to God.

   Job's friends fail him when they give him up for dead. If

they had continued to walk away from his anguished cry, it might have been the end. Ironically, they may have saved him by turning back and contesting his cry. Job still has something to live for because he has something to prove. So often, our will to live in times of stress is created by adversaries who want to see us defeated and dead.

Not long ago, I went through a crisis which my adversaries turned into an issue of my survival. Their tactic backfired. Once I knew that my survival was at stake, I found untapped resources upon which to draw. Just this week a student said, "I see confidence in your countenance. You minister to me." We must never underestimate the capacity of human beings to survive.

When human survival is threatened by outside forces, the will to live can give us a strength never known before. Job's gritty refusal to give up hope is a reminder that even when the threat to life is spiritualized, we have untapped resources upon which to draw.

The Man of Sorrows

Job's friends fail him because they give up too soon, listen too little, and spiritualize too easily. Jesus suffers a similar fate at the hands of His family and friends. When Isaiah envisions Jesus as "a man of sorrows" he puts the description in the context of Jesus being "despised and rejected by men" (Isa. 53:3). Members of His family give up too soon on Him. When friends came to them reporting Jesus' radical statements about His divine identity and His redemptive mission, the family reacts with embarrassment: "He is out of His mind" (Mark 3:21).

Time and time again, Jesus introduces or concludes His teaching with the admonition, "He who has ears to hear, let him hear." He is appealing for an understanding of the meaning of His words over and above admiration of His authoritative style. Of course, those whose security and authority are threatened by His teaching turn their attack into a spiritual confrontation. By exposing the pious protocol upon which the Pharisees rely, Jesus undercuts their personal security and their religious authority. Not unexpectedly, then, they

charge Him with heresy and blasphemy against the Church
and with treason and sedition against the State. As if this
were not enough, their spiritual attack climaxes with the out-
rageous claim that Jesus is in league with the devil!

Of course, Jesus' closest friends also give up on Him too
soon when they abandon Him in the Garden or the palace
courtyard. Despite all the hours He spent with them trying
to convey the promise of the Resurrection, they never hear
the meaning of His message. And, despite the flashes of spiritual insight that came to the disciples during their time with
Jesus, they still doubt Him and cower in fear until the day of
Pentecost.

Because we now know how friends fail us in our suffering, we also know how they help us. If our families and
friends stay with us during our suffering and never give up
hope, we will not despair. If they listen for the meaning of
our cries, we will know a love that accepts us as we are. If
they respond to our needs rather than spiritualizing our anguish, we will have a chance to grow in faith.

In the midst of his suffering, Job reverses roles with his
three friends for just a moment. Initially, he reacts against
them as they have reacted against him:

> I also could speak as you *do,*
> If your soul were in my soul's place.
> I could heap up words against you,
> And shake my head at you.
> (Job 16:4)

Then, out of the insight of his anguish comes the response which he hoped his friends would give:

> But I would strengthen you
>   with my mouth,
> And the comfort of my lips would
>   relieve your grief.
> (Job 16:5)

When we suffer and ask "Why?" there is no substitute
for the special ministry of friends.

"Behold, happy is the man
whom God corrects . . . ."
—Eliphaz

6
How Religion Falters

When we suffer, we turn to religion. With good reason. Only religion can answer our questions:

> Does God care?
> Can I be healed?
> If I die, will I live again?

Human philosophies provide no answer to these questions other than cynicism. When Walter Lippman, a champion of humanism, was asked to sum up his philosophy of life and death, he answered, "Just do the best you can, and if possible, face death with a smile."

Religion is more than facing death with a smile. It is the human way of communicating with God and interpreting His revelation. It is right that we turn to religion when we suffer. We need the comfort of knowing that Someone above and beyond us understands and cares. Of course, every religion requires an element of faith because the answers do not come easily. In fact, they may not come at all. Job had no answers to his suffering when he spoke through faith, "Though He slay me, yet will I trust Him" (Job 13:15).

In such times, the crucial question is, "Does our religion give us the faith to handle suffering even when we do not have all the answers?"

Job's suffering tested the religion that he shared with his three friends, Eliphaz, Bildad, and Zophar. Even though they lived in a time of limited revelation, they had a personal and practical faith in God. It began with natural revelation. In the beauty and order of the physical world, Job and his friends saw the hand of a personal God. At the same time, the awesome evidence of His power caused them to quake with fear. Bowing in His presence and before His power, they arose to sing psalms of praise unsurpassed in poetic beauty and spiritual insight:

> But as for me, I would seek God,
> And to God I would commit my
> cause—
> Who does great things,
> and unsearchable,
> Marvelous things without number.
>
> He gives rain on the earth,
> And sends waters on the fields,
> He sets on high those who are lowly,
> And those who mourn are lifted
> to safety.
> (Eliphaz—Job 5:8–11)

In this hymn which Eliphaz quoted for Job we see that he and his friends represent a religion involving far more than fear of the Almighty and submission to His power. Their God is honored for His justice and praised for His providence. Still more, through the searching of human reason, they have been inspired to an understanding of "wisdom" whose definition remains intact throughout the Scriptures. By worshiping God in fear and submitting their minds to His will, they believed they would gain a wisdom that permitted them "to see God whole" and understand His ways in the world. Their view of wisdom, however, was not just a lofty ideal without practical application. For them, wisdom also meant "to walk circumspectly" before God. This was the model of wisdom and righteousness that Job exemplified and God commended: ". . . a blameless and upright man, one who fears God and shuns evil?" (Job 1:8).

We continue to be amazed at the high level of spiritual insight and practical righteousness that Job and his friends espoused without the advantage of God's special revelation through the Law and the Prophets or through the Incarnation of Jesus Christ. Never sell them short. Better yet, never sell short the Spirit of God. Hebrews reminds us that even before the revelation of Jesus Christ, God was working in "various times and in different ways" (Heb. 1:1) to reveal His will and His love to His human creation.

Religion, however, can be too perfect sometimes. In trying to become wise and live righteously, Job and his friends tried to answer every question and cover every contingency with a reasonable religious explanation. The more they explained, the less faith they needed. Therefore, they fell into the trap of reducing faith to a formula, raising the formula to a system, and finally substituting the system for faith itself. This is a vicious cycle that allows no room for growth in faith. When this happens, especially for people who suffer and ask "Why?", religion falters.

When Faith Is Reduced to a Formula

Believe it or not, religion can be detrimental to faith. If this happens, religion actually adds to the pain of people who suffer. Job's friends illustrate what we mean. In their zeal to understand God, they reduced faith to a formula. The result was a religion that took the mystery out of life, answered the question "Why?" for all circumstances, and eliminated the need for a faith that is ". . . the substance of things hoped for, the evidence of things not seen" (Heb. 11:1). With the surety of physical law, they developed the spiritual equation:

Sin equals suffering;

Righteousness equals prosperity.

Each premise is true. Whether in the Old or New Testament, the lesson is taught that the "wages of sin is death." Likewise, we cannot deny the truth that "Righteousness exalts a nation, but sin is a reproach to any people" (Prov. 14:34). But what happens when you meet a person like Job?

He suffers even though he is righteous. Suddenly, the formula is tested and fails. Justice, of course, makes no provision for such exceptions. Like ringing up a sale on a cash register, if you punch in sin, suffering is your change. Everything in the world of Eliphaz, Bildad, and Zophar worked like that. No exceptions were allowed. Faith went with the formula and God's character went with the faith. Job is caught in the middle, a righteous man who is suffering, crying "Why?", and needing a faith that gives him hope. Indeed, he is condemned as a sinner because his circumstances do not fit the formula. Crossing the lines of the equation, he is a contradiction because he is a righteous man who suffers.

Faith is still being reduced to formulas. If we are honest we will confess that when we suffer, we not only ask "Why?" but also, "What have I done wrong?" In our minds we link sin and suffering. Likewise, in our affluent society, we want to link our riches with our righteousness. How else can we account for the popularity of the preaching that promises prosperity and success for those who obey God? In its extreme form, there is even a preacher who boldly proclaims the idea that "the lack of money is the root of all evil." Most Christians would categorically reject such a perversion of the gospel, but not necessarily the formula behind it. Winston Churchill once said that the only thing wrong with Christianity is the lack of suffering. In his own way, he was right. We do not know how to handle either success or suffering.

New Christians are particularly susceptible to the righteousness/prosperity side of the Wisdom School formula. Naturally ecstatic with their new-found freedom in Christ, they believe that nothing can go wrong. While discussing a tragic death in a Christian family, a young mother who had been marvelously converted offered this testimony, "I have no fear for our family. We have claimed the promise of the blood on the doorpost. Nothing can happen to our children." How would she handle the suffering of Job?

In another instance of faith reduced to a formula in the mind of a new Christian, I chanced to sit next to a young woman on an airplane who was reading C. S. Lewis's *The Chronicles of Narnia*. Curiously, I asked her if she had read many of his works. "Some," she answered. "I'm a new Christian and I'm just becoming acquainted with him." She went on to explain how Christ had changed her life and given her success after success in the music business as a vocalist in Broadway-type musicals. Together, then, we talked about our mutual faith and C. S. Lewis's insightful writing. When she inquired about other of his works to help her growth in faith, I recommended his primer *Mere Christianity,* his autobiography *Surprised by Joy,* and his Jobian struggle through suffering after the death of his wife, *A Grief Observed.*

As the plane landed, we agreed to continue our conversation by correspondence. Several months passed before I heard from her. The first page of her letter bubbled with the good news of God at work in her life. But the second page reflected her troubled spirit. She felt "disillusioned" after reading *A Grief Observed* because she could not accept Lewis's angry yell:

> So this is what God is really like.
> Deceive yourself no longer.

Nor could she reconcile her concept of God and faith with Lewis's conclusion:

> She smiled, but not at me. *Poi si torno all'*
> *eterna fontana.* [1]

My young friend has yet to suffer. When she does, I have no doubt but that her desire to grow as a Christian will be honored by the Holy Spirit. Hers will be an expanding, maturing faith that understands the anguish and the ending of C. S. Lewis's experience. As of now, however, her Christianity is encapsulated in a formula of prosperity and success that makes no room for suffering.

When the Formula Is Raised to a System

Once faith is reduced to a formula, it is the formula, not the faith, that must be defended. How creative we now become. Every human invention is brought into play, especially human experience, tradition, and reason. In contemporary

---

[1]*Translation:* "Seeing that indeed round and round the eternal fountain (flows)."

terms, we call it systematic theology—meaning that the revelation of God is organized, explained, and defended by scholarly work. As a leader of the Wisdom School, Job undoubtedly had a hand in developing the formula for faith and its supporting theological system. He respected the wisdom of human experience, tradition, and reason. Little did he know, however, that his own work would be used as a weapon against him when his friends tried to prove that his suffering resulted from some form of sin.

Eliphaz, the eldest and therefore presumed to be the wisest of Job's three friends, defended the formula of faith by invoking the authority of his age and the *experience of a nighttime vision* when God spoke personally to him:

> Then a spirit passed before my face . . .
> Then I heard a voice saying:
> "Can a mortal be more righteous
> than God?
> Can a man be more pure
> than His maker?
> If He puts no trust in His servants,
> If He charges His angels with error,
> How much more those who dwell
> in houses of clay?"
>
> (Job 4:15–19)

Eliphaz puts Job in an impossible position. Who can dispute the wisdom of age? Who can refute the infallibility of a secret, supernatural vision? Although Eliphaz's tone is fatherly, he minces no words in diagnosing Job's suffering as the result of sin and prescribing repentance:

> Behold, happy is the man
> whom God corrects;
> Therefore, do not despise the
> chastening of the Almighty . . . .
>
> Behold, this we have searched out;
> It is true.
> Hear it and know for yourself.
>
> (Job 5:17 and 27)

In his turn, Bildad reinforces Eliphaz's position by citing the *tradition of the fathers* in defense of the formula. Job is again forced into an impossible situation because he has taught others that the accumulated understanding of the ages is essential to wisdom. Bildad's words must have stung Job deeply when he invoked tradition as his authority for defending the formula and condemning Job:

> For inquire, please, of the former age,
> And consider the things discovered
>   by their fathers;
> For we were born yesterday,
>   and know nothing.
>
> (Job 8:8–9)

Having established his authority in the wisdom of the ancients, Bildad spins three parables which must have been passed down from generation to generation as reinforcements for the formula—the papyrus reed that withers without water, the spider whose web collapses under his weight, and the gourd that rots because of shallow roots. Each parable has the same pointed moral. Job is suffering because of secret sin in his life.

Zophar is the third speaker. He builds his case for the formula by resorting to the *logic of human reason* which Job respected and mastered. Like a debater refuting the case of an opponent, Zophar quotes Job's own words and turns them against him:

> For you have said,
> "My doctrine is pure,
> And I am clean in your eyes."
> But oh, that God would speak,
> And open His lips against you,
> That He would show you the secrets
>   of wisdom!
> For they would double your prudence.
> Know therefore that God exacts from
>   you
> *Less than your iniquity deserves.*
>
> (Job 11:4–6, emphasis mine)

Job is caught in a crossfire of condemnation. To protect their formula for faith, his three friends turn legitimate sources of support for divine revelation into tactics of terror. By appealing to the authority of experience, tradition, and reason which Job respects, they leave him no alternative but repentance before God or rebellion against Him. Thus, God's justice will be defended, their formula will be preserved, and they themselves will be vindicated. Meanwhile, Job's suffering deepens as he is sacrificed for the system.

When the System Replaces Faith

A vicious cycle came to an end when Job's three friends substituted their system of theology for faith itself. Once they began to create a theology with all of the answers, momentum carried them to the point where Job no longer mattered. Eliphaz, Bildad, and Zophar were so intent on defending their religious system that they were viciously compelled to find sin in Job's life. When Eliphaz could not identify any obvious sin, Bildad presumed that the problem was secret sin. Still without evidence, Zophar tried to get Job to plea bargain with God because he knew that his suffering is less than he deserves for his sin.

The contest continues until Eliphaz latches on to the angry words of Job and accuses him of sinning with his tongue. Later on, Bildad shifts the ground rules from searching for a specific sin in Job's life to damning his total character. In one of the most precise profiles in Scripture of the wicked person, Bildad throws out personalized barbs that can apply only to Job, involving the loss of his family, fame, and fortune. Through clenched teeth, Bildad stabs a finger in Job's direction and cuts him to the quick with his indictment:

> The light of the wicked
> indeed goes out . . . .
> And this is the place of him
> who does not know God.
> (Job 18:5 and 21)

Desperation has taken over. Even Eliphaz loses his suave and fatherly diplomacy when he shouts, in paraphrase:

> *So what if you are innocent?*
> *Is it any pleasure to the Almighty*
> *that you are righteous?*

With one last dig, Eliphaz then accuses Job of being guilty of the sins of the rich:

. . . taking pledges from a brother without reason,
. . . stripping the naked of their clothing,
. . . refusing water to the weary,
. . . withholding bread from the hungry,
. . . sending widows away empty, and
. . . crushing the strength of the fatherless.

(Job 22:6–9)

Point for point, Job refutes these charges and, in fact, shows how he went the extra mile in each case. Nothing is left to attack. In utter desperation, Bildad admits their failure when he sniffs at Job:

How much less man, who is a maggot,
And a son of man, who is a worm?
(Job 25:6)

There is no mistaking the object of his invective. Bildad closes the conversation by consigning Job to the rank of a worm in the dust or a maggot grubbing in a rotting corpse. Think of it. Under the pretense of defending the character of God, Job had fallen in the eyes of Eliphaz, Bildad, and Zophar from a friend to be comforted, to a sinner to be censured, to a wicked person to be damned, and finally to a worm to be trampled. It all began when faith was reduced to a formula.

A Victim of the System

The parallel between the suffering of Job and Jesus at the hands of religious leaders is astounding. Jesus' opposition came from Pharisees who reduced faith to a formula that equated righteousness with ritual. Around that formula, the Pharisees developed an institutionalized system of hundreds of petty rules for righteousness. Somewhere under the weight of those rules faith got lost. Therefore, when Jesus came preaching faith in God as the essence of spirituality, the Pharisees took the same tactic as Job's friends, attacking Jesus under the pretense of defending the character of God.

Note the similarity of vicious cycles. When the Pharisees realized that Jesus' message threatened their power and position, they resorted to a personalized attack—scoffing at His ancestry, denying His legitimacy, implying His madness, and aligning Him with Beelzebub. Nothing worked. Jesus stood firm in His message and pure in His character. Enraged by their failure to accuse Him, the Pharisees plotted His death—to stomp Him out like a worm or a maggot.

Philippians reminds us that Jesus, the Son of God, relinquished His glory to be born a man, ministered as a servant, suffered the loss of reputation, and died as a criminal. With Him as well as with Job, it all began when faith was reduced to a formula, the formula was raised to a system, and the system replaced the value of a person, even one in the midst of suffering.

For those who suffer, the experience of Jesus and Job is a reminder that religion can be cruel as well as comforting. Religious formulas and systems can add to our pain if they become substitutes for faith itself. In such instances, we must tenaciously hold on to our faith in God at all costs. He is not threatened by our anguished cries or our troubled thoughts. Even though He may not answer immediately, He will not abandon us. Best of all, God will never deny our dignity as persons even when we feel as if we are on an ashheap. Job and Jesus assure us that He hurts with us, hears us, and will heal us, not always as we may wish, but always with new faith that gives us hope.

"When He has tested me,
I will come forth as gold."
—Job

7
How Faith Grows

Faith can grow during the time when we must suffer and ask "Why?" None of us would choose to suffer in order to grow in faith. Just the opposite. Our natural instinct is to avoid pain and shy away from suffering. Even if we were given the choice between suffering and health at the expense of a growing faith, we would choose health. Why not? Church history is replete with people who pursued suffering as the path to spirituality. Seekers of suffering range all the way from "flagellantes" in the Philippines who beat themselves with whips to "hypochondriacs" in the United States who manipulate their physical ills to spiritual advantage. At either extreme, those who seek suffering end up scarred but no more saintly than those who pursue health with equal vigor.

Still, we cannot deny the growing faith of those who suffer. Television brings us story after story of persons who are victims of deadly diseases, crippling accidents, and vicious crimes. Almost without exception, those who suffer find resources within themselves not just to bear their suffering but faith to encourage others. This morning's paper carries the story of a football coach who has the incurable

75

Lou Gehrig's disease which attacks the nervous system. Even though his prognosis is grim, the coach is on the field with his team, one arm dangling helplessly at his side, the other in a sling. His voice is reduced to a whisper so that the players have to strain their ears to hear his command, "O.K. Let's be happy and go hard." Inspired by his courage, team members say, "When he talks, everybody listens."

Who has not been inspired and shamed by similar stories of suffering people? Our first reaction is that we do not see how they can face such circumstances. Then we see them smile and speak of a sustaining faith that we have never known. Envy almost takes over. We breathe a silent prayer that our faith might be as strong. Yet we know deep within ourselves that such faith will not come without the test of suffering.

Job mirrors the image of our lives. Like him, we cruise through life taking health and prosperity for granted until suffering takes us by surprise. In a moment of time, our faith is put to the test. After exhausting ourselves crying "Why?", desperation causes us to reach for resources upon which we have never drawn and about which we have never known.

Suffering presses our faith in God to its outer limits— and beyond. When our suffering is total and our current faith is inadequate, the only alternative is to grow in faith or lapse back into futility. Job's suffering put him in this position. He did not make a conscious or courageous choice to suffer in order to grow in faith. In fact, it was all he could do to hang on to the faith he had. Yet, his doggedness put him on the growth line toward a maturing faith. The process is painful but infinitely worthwhile.

Faith Grows on Faith

Each of us brings to suffering the faith that we already have. It is false to assume that a person without faith in God will suddenly come to faith through suffering. Faith may come, but it will be most elementary. Likewise it is false to assume that suffering will spontaneously produce a spurt of mature faith in a spiritual neophyte. Faith may grow, but it will be a step at a time. I learned this lesson as a chaplain in a hospital. Answering a call for ministry, I visited a diabetic who had just had one foot amputated. As I approached his bed, I saw the other foot outside the bed sheets so that an open, running sore could be exposed to the air. Gangrene, which had caused one foot to be amputated, threatened the other as well. His doctors had asked if I would help them convince the patient to follow the hygienic precautions which he had ignored. Otherwise, his foot and his life were in jeopardy.

I intended to ease into the conversation, but the patient charged at me with a declaration of his faith. A year earlier, he told me, he had traveled over 500 miles to the revival meeting of a faith healer who touched him and pronounced him healed of his diabetes. Even though the patient was not a professing Christian, he put his faith in the healer and stopped following his doctor's orders for medication and cleanliness. Thus, he lost one foot and endangered the other.

After I had gained his confidence by daily visits and listening, I discreetly asked if he sensed any contradiction between his faith in the healer and his loss of a foot. With firm resolution, he answered, "No. I would travel 500 miles to be touched by him again." The lesson is sad, but true. Through the desperation of suffering, a man without faith in God put his trust in a faith healer who supposedly represented God. The nature of his faith, however, was so elementary that it was unrealistic. His faith was a fantasy that eventually cost him both feet and, ultimately, his life.

The faith a person brings to suffering determines how faith can grow through that suffering. In his book, *The Stages of Faith Development,* James Fowler identifies six levels of faith through which we can grow a step at a time.

I. *Intuitive-Projective Faith*—a child's faith based upon fantasy and imagination.
II. *Mythical-Literal Faith*—early childhood/family faith based upon moral rules and either-or thinking.
III. *Synthetic-Conventional Faith*—adolescent faith based upon the tradition of the community and imitation of faith models.

IV. *Individuative-Reflective Faith*—young adult faith based upon critical, reflective, and independent thinking.

V. *Conjunctive Faith*—a midlife and old-age faith based upon the integration of self-identity with a comprehensive world view which leads to serving and being served.

VI. *Universalizing Faith*—a rare faith based upon a transcendent vision which leads to a disciplined, active and self-giving life.[1]

Each of us can find the level of faith that is foundational for our life. If we are honest, we will even admit fluctuation between the levels of faith from time to time. In some circumstances, the maturity of our faith astounds us as we give ourselves in unselfish service to others. In other circumstances, we are shamed by the low level of our faith as we regress to fantasy and imagination. What makes the difference? Most likely it is the extent to which the circumstances threaten us. I, for instance, can exercise universalizing or self-giving faith when I envision the future of the seminary I serve. Yet for my own career, I keep falling back to the lowest level of faith, indulging in fantasy and barely able to trust God.

Job teaches us that suffering forces us to locate the foundational level of our faith. As we noted earlier, the Wisdom School which Job and his friends represented claimed a faith based upon critical thinking and reflective reasoning. In truth, however, they had reduced faith to a formula based upon the either-or equation:

> Sin equals suffering;
>
> Righteousness equals prosperity.

Around this formula, then, they developed a religious system that relied upon intuition, tradition, and imitation for support. Again, we see that Job and his friends are not people of little faith. In their search for God, they had progressed to the reflective level of faith—fashioned out of sound reasoning and applied in practical righteousness.

Job illustrates how Reflective Faith sustained him during the calamities that wiped out his fortune, fame and family. With chilling logic, he responds:

> The Lord gives, the Lord takes away,
> Blessed be the name of the Lord.

His Reflective Faith was equal to the test. I, however, have confessed that I would have a hard time being so glib about the loss of my meager fortune and magnificent family. Maybe I am revealing that I have a lower level of faith which cannot handle such tragedy. Or perhaps I am revealing that the level of my faith has not been tested by such circumstances. Still, as I reach down, down, down to the bedrock of my trust in God, I feel as if I would be able to discover resources of faith upon which I have never drawn before. If so, my faith would grow under test.

This was the case with Job. When Satan attacked him personally, took away his health, and subjected him to total suffering, certain questions emerged. Would Job grow in faith to the Conjunctive Level where faith becomes larger than the sum of its parts? Or would Job attain the Universalizing Level of faith that permits him to see through to God and give himself away in selfless service?

Faith Grows through Struggle

Faith does not grow on a smooth path along a straight line. Anyone who thinks that the walk of faith is an idyllic journey has never been tested by intense suffering. A better picture for the walk of faith is given to us by Elliott Wright in his book, *The Holy Company.* Tracing the biographies of eighty persons whom history has identified as "saints," Elliott discovers that they are a diverse company of peculiar people with only one thing in common. Each has an insatiable thirst for God which keeps them "hobbling" toward holiness.[2]

In recent days, I have developed my own visual image for the test of faith. God seems to have put me on a "yo-yo" of highs and lows that are both spiritually confusing and emotionally exhausting. On successive days, He has taken me from the exhilarating high of a multi-million-dollar endowment for the seminary to the humiliating low of what I interpreted as a personal repudiation by a friend. One day later, my ego got a stratospheric boost when my name flashed across the television screen as a potential presidential candidate on a CBS news special hosted by Walter Cronkite. Within twenty-four hours, however, I sank back into self-doubt when my name was omitted from a long and obvious list of evangelical Christian leaders.

More than once during a week when I rode up and down on a yo-yo string, I asked God, "Why?" and "What are You doing to me?" The answer came back, "Trust Me." So, exercising rare patience, I have tried to hold steady and learn what God is trying to teach me.

Patience pays off. At the bottom of the yo-yo string, I see His promise to take me through new and changing circumstances; at the top, I envision His promise for a bright and challenging future. I still don't like the highs and lows of riding on a yo-yo string, but I must confess that my faith has been extended to new dimensions of spiritual insight which I have never encountered before.

Faith Grows by Steps

Job rode the yo-yo too. We tend to emphasize either his "ups" of faith or his "downs" of suffering. A careful reading of the story with a particular sensitivity to the highs and lows of his experience in suffering will show us the connection between the two.

On the *low side* of Job's suffering, we see him sinking lower and lower into despair until his cries of anguish turn bitter and border on blasphemy. His own words take us down, down, down into the depths of despair with him:

NO HOPE IN LIFE:
   "Why did I not die at birth?" (3:11)
   NO HOPE IN SELF:
      "How can a man be righteous before God?" (9:2)
      NO HOPE IN FRIENDS:
         "Will you contend for God?" (13:8)
         NO HOPE IN DEATH:
            "If a man dies, shall he live again?" (14:4)
            NO HOPE IN GOD:
               "How long will You torment my soul?"
(19:2)

Teenagers describe the times when they are down as being in "the pits." Few of us, however, ever fathom the depth of the pit into which Job sank. At most we may give up on life, ourselves, and our friends. But still, we hold our hope in life after death and in the mercy of God.

Job does not give up. He keeps asking questions with the hope of some answer that will lift him up from despair. Remember that he lived in a time before God had revealed the concept of eternal life to people of faith. So, Job juggles fatalism with faith in his question, "If a man dies, shall he live again?" Hoping against hope, he must have had some premonition that death is not the end. For instance, God seems to be a silent adversary tearing at his body, mind, and soul. Still Job asks, "How long will you torment my soul . . . ?" In his question is the untested assumption that sooner or later God will lift His hand and save His servant's soul.

As difficult as it may seem for a suffering person who is sinking lower and lower into the pit of despair, God still says, "Trust Me." People who have not established an earlier trust relationship with God will find it especially hard to keep their faith while sinking. Yet, even a smidgen of trust can be strengthened by the grace that God promises for our times of testing.

Up to the Pinnacle

Job's experience on the *high side* of faith proves the point. As you read his long and labored complaints against God, the sense of futility seems overwhelming. But then, each time he hits a new low, faith takes hold in a flash of prophetic insight which comes to him through the Spirit of God. Follow the rising action as Job sees beyond his time through faith:

HOPE IN THE CHRIST OF GOD
"I know that my Redeemer lives . . ."
(19:25)

HOPE IN THE LIFE OF GOD
"If a man dies, shall he live again?"
(14:14)

HOPE IN THE FRIENDSHIP OF GOD
"Though He slay me, yet will I trust Him."
(13:15)

HOPE IN THE MERCY OF GOD
"Your hands have made me and fashioned me,
An intricate unity; Yet You would destroy me."
(10:8)

HOPE IN THE JUSTICE OF GOD
"God is wise in heart and mighty in strength."
(9:4)

In this image of rising action, we see faith growing toward maturity through the struggle of suffering. Like mountain peaks projecting out of the fog which covers the valleys below, Job's breakthroughs of faith rise higher and higher until he stands on the pinnacle of faith and makes the prophetic declaration:

> For I know that my Redeemer lives,
> And He shall stand at last on the
>   earth;
> And after my skin is destroyed,
>   this I know,
> That in my flesh I shall see God.
> (Job 19:25–26)

This lofty declaration of faith is the *turning point* in the Book of Job. From now on, Job takes the initiative in the debate with his friends. And even though he lapses back into despair from time to time, the sinking ceases and the tenor of his talk takes on a strength that permits him to focus on the issue of his innocence rather than upon personal attacks against either his friends or God.

Faith grows like that. In our struggle with deepening despair caused by suffering, the Spirit of God breaks through with flashes of spiritual insight that become more profound as we hold our trust in God. Yet we must remember that Job did not rise to the pinnacle of faith without those moments of floundering in the pit of futility. Therefore, the picture of a growing faith is like a musical crescendo in which the falling line of futility is matched by the rising line of faith until the grand note of faith is sounded to set the tone for the music to follow. In graphic protrayal, we see the crescendo of Job's growing faith:

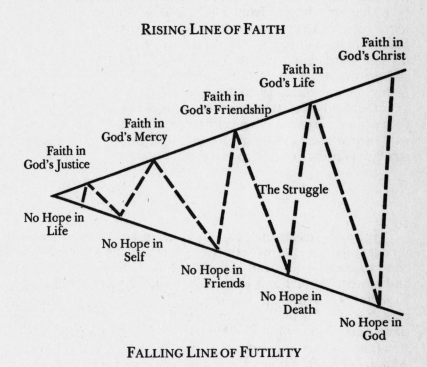

RISING LINE OF FAITH

Faith in God's Christ

Faith in God's Life

Faith in God's Friendship

Faith in God's Mercy

Faith in God's Justice

The Struggle

No Hope in Life

No Hope in Self

No Hope in Friends

No Hope in Death

No Hope in God

FALLING LINE OF FUTILITY

When all is said and done, Job's hope is our hope. From the pinnacle of faith, he foresees the Atonement of Christ our Redeemer, the Incarnation of Christ who became flesh and lived among us, and the Resurrection of Christ who gives us our only hope for eternal life. Think of it. Job, the man who lived before the time of the Law or the Prophets, affirms his faith in the promises of God which are yet to be revealed! By holding to his trust through the struggle of his suffering, Job came to see God's view of the final Revelation on which he can rest his hope.

Suffering people shame us with their prophetic insights into the future that God has for us. One of my dearest friends lay dying of cancer. In his long and lonely hours of insufferable pain, I expected to find him severely depressed. Instead, he said to me on my last visit before his death, "I'm so glad that I lived my life in the world of ideas. Not even cancer can take that world away from me." As you would expect, his mind came more and more alive as his body died. Family and friends hung on his every word, not just because it might be his last word, but because his spiritual and intellectual insights were never so profound. Despite the depth of his suffering, he was seeing from the pinnacle of faith!

Our faith grows the same way. Out of our greatest struggles with the contradictions of human existence, faith makes its greatest gains. Faith grows on faith; faith grows out of struggle; faith grows a step at a time.

The Pit and the Pinnacle

Jesus also experienced the growth of faith through suffering. Like Job and us, His life appears to be a bundle of contradictions—God and Man, Divine and Human, Sufferer and Savior, Servant and King, Glory and Shame, Death and Resurrection. Although He frequently cried out to His disciples, "O you of little faith," and repudiated the Pharisees for their pretensions of faith, He Himself went through the struggle of faith in preparation for His death on the cross. Alone, He stood on the highest pinnacle of faith when He trusted God to bring Him through the suffering of death and hell into resurrection of the body with the assurance of eternal life.

In Christ we see the potential of our faith. From the pit of hell, He arose with the shout, "Behold, I am alive, now and evermore." In that supreme moment of divine and human history, Jesus Christ shows us the meaning of a faith in which a transcendent vision is enacted in a self-giving Person. As rare as it may be, we too can rise to the pinnacle of faith. Suffering may be the cost, but the witness of such faith is eternally worthwhile.

8
How Love Holds

When we suffer and ask "Why?", only love can hold us. Job was introduced to us as a man who lived in a time of limited revelation, embraced a religion based upon fear, and claimed a righteousness built upon self-discipline. Now we meet him as a person who also enjoyed a relationship with God that went far beyond submission and servitude. God Himself reveals that relationship when He asks Satan, "Have you considered My servant Job, . . . a blameless and upright man, one who fears God and shuns evil?" (Job 1:8). A world of meaning is evident in the words, ". . . My servant Job." God is saying:

> I call him by his name,
> I claim him as My friend,
> I commend him as My servant.

What a compliment! It is exceeded only by the parallel passage in the Gospels when God affirms Jesus at His baptism, "This is My beloved Son, in Whom I am well pleased" (Mark 1:11).

If I had only one sermon to preach, I would choose this text from the Gospel of Mark. In it are all the essentials of the relationship that I desire of God for myself and others. Simply put, God claims Jesus as His Son whom He loves and of whom He is proud. Jesus needs nothing more for His sense of identity, His sense of security, and His feeling of worth. God says to His Son, "You belong to Me, I love you, and I am proud of you."

Extending this truth to my own life, I too realize that I need nothing more. To belong, to be loved, and to be praised by God is the highest commendation I can know. Therefore, to those who would hear the sermon of my life, I would speak with utter confidence—God claims us, loves us, and wants to praise us as His sons and daughters.

Here again we see the prophetic leaning of the Book of Job toward Jesus Christ in God's commendation, "Have you considered My servant Job?" His words confirm a personal relationship which goes beyond fear-filled worship and disciplined righteousness. God claims, loves, and praises Job as a son, a friend, and a servant. The relationship is mutual. The way in which Job talks to God is possible only in the confidence of mutual love.

As he gropes for the "Why?" Job dares to tease God as one might banter with a close friend. More than that, he takes the risk of testing Him as a covenant brother who seems to have turned upon him without reason. Yet, despite a prolonged monologue that begins with a tease and ends with a demand for justice, Job never loses his trust in God as his Father. Even though he does not hear God's question to Satan, he intuitively senses its meaning.

"Have you considered My servant Job?" reveals God's side of a love relationship—claiming him, loving him, and praising him. On Job's side, he knows that he belongs to God, is loved by Him, and is praised by Him. Even total and grotesque suffering cannot take away his *identity* as a son, his *security* as a friend, and his *worth* as a servant. Love holds Job through his suffering.

Teasing Love

Among the many hints of the love relationship between God and Job, one stands out as unique. In his first rebuttal of Eliphaz's charge that he is a sinner who must repent, Job's anger turns to grief because his friends have failed him. After scolding them for their lack of understanding, he turns to God and addresses Him directly for the first time. Anguish pours from Job's heart and at the bottom is not bitterness, but the most profound question in scripture:

> WHAT IS MAN,
>   that You should exalt him,
> That You should set Your heart on
>   him,
> That You should visit him every
>   morning,
> And test him every moment?
> How long?
> Will You not look away from me,
> And let me alone till I swallow my
>   saliva?
> Have I sinned?
> What have I done to You,
>   O watcher of men?
> Why have You set me as Your target,
> So that I am a burden to myself?
> Why then do You not pardon my
>   transgression,
> And take away my iniquity?
> For now I will lie down in the dust,
> And You will seek me diligently,
> But I will no longer be.
>
>   (Job 7:17–21)

This is Job's psalm of suffering. Anyone who suffers will identify with his questions and the lack of answers. But wait. There is a love note hidden in the woeful song. Based upon their past relationship as friends, Job chides God with a reminder of what He will lose if Job dies:

> And You will seek me diligently,
> But I will no longer be.

Lovers tease each other by saying, "You'll miss me when I'm gone." Even when it is said in jest, it's true. The loss of loved ones leaves us with a hollow heart. Going into a room, we expect them to be there. Calling out their name, we expect them to answer. Reaching out for them, we expect their touch. The loss of a loved one is irreparable for both parties.

How does Job dare to tease God by saying, "You'll miss me when I'm gone"? If he is not a partner in a love relationship, his arrogance is unforgivable. Try the same question with a stranger or an enemy. Without an intimate knowledge of each other's sensitivities, teasing must be avoided at all cost.

I have a friend who lost his thumb and three fingers on his left hand from a childhood accident with a dynamite cap. The first time I met him, nothing was said about his hand because neither of us knew how the other would respond to the handicap. In our next meeting, however, he told me the story of the accident. Later, I heard that students in the college where he coached called him "Uncle Nubby." Still later, I heard him speak at a banquet where he brought the house down with "Twenty-nine stories on how I got my nub."

Slowly and with extreme caution, I tested whether I could tease him about his nubby hand. Bit by bit a developing and deepening relationship stood the test of teasing. Soon I was introducing him as "Uncle Nubby" to student groups and adding my own absurd version to his twenty-nine stories. He himself led the laughter and when his time came, returned my teasing with some kind of comment that implied, "You'll miss me when I'm gone." He's right, even in jest. Underneath the teasing is a friendship whose loss would leave a hollow spot.

Job dares to tease God the same way. He cannot be accused of arrogance or irreverence. Rather, on the basis of a loving relationship that permitted God to test Job and Job to tease God, he said, "You'll miss me when I'm gone." Only love can say that.

Testing Love

God does not respond to Job's teasing. His silence confounds His friend. Job realizes now that he is suffering not only the loss of God's protection, but also the loss of His voice, and with it the promise of His word. Verbal communication is essential to any love relationship. Although friends and lovers can communicate without words, the moments of silence grow out of hours of intimate conversation. The communication of silence, in fact, can take place only between people who have first communicated through words. Otherwise, the silence is awkward and embarrassing.

Two strangers cannot sit in silence without talking unless they choose to ignore each other's presence, if not each other's existence. On airplanes if I am seated next to a stranger, for instance, I have the choice of opening a conversation or blocking the small space between our seats by silence. If I choose to open the conversation, I usually become involved in the life of the other person and, therefore, find it difficult to lapse back into my reading or writing. So, if I need to read, write, or think, I say "hello" and then proceed to open a book, take out a pad, or close my eyes as a signal that I don't want to talk.

When I travel with my wife, however, it is just the opposite. We can enjoy each other without speaking. She knows that I frequently read, write, or think while flying. Therefore, with just an occasional touch of the hand we communicate. Out of the experience of past conversation and the assurance of future conversation, we are comfortable in silence. Each of us knows that when the other needs to talk, we will be ready to listen and respond.

But what if the conversation between two lovers ceases? Something has to be wrong. The first assumption is that silence is the result of inattention or preoccupation. Teasing, such as "You'll miss me when I'm gone," usually takes care of that. No answer? Naturally, the ignored person assumes that he or she has done something wrong. "What have I done to hurt you?" is a common question between friends and lovers whose communication has been mysteriously broken off.

But what if the person still doesn't speak? The appeal advances to a call for a rational approach to the problem, such as, "Give me a reason why you won't talk to me." If this appeal fails, the final recourse is to go public by asking for an open hearing, such as, "Will you go to a counselor with me?"

or "Can we ask friends to help us?" Only in the most desperate circumstances do friends and lovers take their case to court. They know that once in the courtroom, they are adversaries. It takes the rarest of love to hold in a confrontational setting where the primary issue has become a question of justice.

Job cannot stand the silence of God. If only his Friend would speak to him once more, he feels as if he could understand his suffering. Instead, the silence of God provokes him to pursue the test of love to the extreme of calling for justice at the risk of losing that love.

At first, Job cannot conceive of himself as entering into a rational argument over his innocence with God. In response to Bildad's demand for his repentance, Job answers:

> Truly I know it is so,
> But how can a man be righteous
>   before God?
> If one wished to contend with Him,
> He could not answer Him
>   one time out of a thousand.
>   (Job 9:2–3)

In a sense, Job is talking to himself. Quite in contrast to his past experience of open and friendly conversation with God, he is asking in his own mind if he dares to challenge God to a debate in order to reopen their conversation. In successive thoughts, Job asks himself:

> How then can I answer Him,
> And choose my words to reason with
>   Him?
>   (Job 9:14)

> I am blameless,
>   yet I do not know myself;
>   (Job 9:21)

> For He is not a man, as I am,
> That I may answer Him,
> And that we should go to court
>   together.
> Nor is there any mediator between us,
> Who may lay his hand on us both.
>   (Job 9:32–33)

God still does not answer. Finally in sheer desperation,
Job concludes that he has nothing to lose in a direct confrontation with God his Friend. He concludes his self-debate by
saying:

> My soul loathes my life;
> I will give free course to my
>   complaint,
> I will speak in bitterness
>   of my soul.
> I will say to God,
>   "Do not condemn me;
> Show me why You contend with me."
>   (Job 10:1–2)

The stage is set for Job to argue with a silent God. With
a boldness that few sufferers would dare to risk, he challenges God:

> Does it seem good to You that You
>   should oppress . . . ?
> Do You have eyes of flesh . . . ?
> And there is no one who can deliver
>   from Your hand . . . ?
> And will You turn me to dust again?
>   (Job 10:3, 4, 7 and 9)

All these questions, admittedly spoken out of the bitterness of his heart, lead Job back to the first question that he
asked:

> Why then have You brought me
>   out of the womb?
>   (Job 10:18)

Job's question hangs in the air. It is a reasonable question
for suffering people to ask. If God really loves His creation,
why does He permit us to suffer? No answer comes. For those
of us who are burdened with guilt, we simply assume that
suffering is fair payment for our sins. With Job, however, his
innocence drives him to demand a courtroom setting in
which a third and neutral party arbitrates the conflict between him and God. He doesn't want to win as much as he
wants to understand why God has targeted him for suffering
and yet remains silent.

The test is on: In preparation for a legal contest, Job makes two formal requests of God. One is that God give him space so that he will not be afraid to speak; the other is that God speak to him once again, either with an accusation that Job can answer or with an answer to Job's questions:

> How many are my iniquities and sins . . . ?
> Why do You hide Your face . . . ?
> (Job 13:23–24)

Job is no longer pleading for either the love of a friend or the mercy of a brother, but for the justice of God. From now on, he is willing to put himself on the scales that weigh our sin against our righteousness. How many of us would dare take that risk? Like Nebuchadnezzar, we would be weighed in the balances and found wanting. Not Job. He is willing to have the motives of his heart and the conduct of his life put on the scales of divine justice and to accept the verdict of an impartial judge.

God still does not answer. Completely baffled, Job exhausts every means of reasonable recourse which he knows. Having hoped for a mediator and having pleaded for a hearing before God, he finally resorts to a call for a public trial to attest his innocence. After writing his own bill of particulars which lists every sin of which he might be accused, Job contends for his innocence and then puts his life on the line:

> Here is my mark.
> Oh, that the Almighty
>   would answer me,
> That my Prosecutor had written a
>   book!
> Surely I would carry it on my shoulder,
> And bind it on me like a crown;
> (Job 31:35–36)

According to the laws of his time, Job's court of last resort is to appear in public with the charges against him written on a tablet to be read by all people as he carries it through the streets of the city. Anyone who can prove his guilt on any count is invited to come forward and press charges. In contest with a silent God, Job is willing to do anything to get his former Friend to speak. He has taken the test of love into the court of last resort!

If Job's tests for God are isolated from a love relationship, they become adversarial acts that border on blasphemy. In fact, Job's three friends interpret his brash and wordy challenges to God as evidence of his sin and wickedness. Why would God permit a human upstart to question His integrity by demanding a courtroom hearing, insisting upon a bill of particulars, and appealing for public vindication? Trusting love is the only answer.

Trusting Love

People who suffer have a ministry all their own. They teach us the meaning of trusting love. For the sake of definition, trusting love is that which holds when all the traditional supports for faith are taken away. Job is our example. In succession, he apparently loses God's *protection* for his life, His *promise* for his future, and His *presence* for his suffering.

Few of us know what it means to have our faith tested without the *protection, promise,* and *presence* of God. Most of our testing is in the shallows of our faith. Illness may seem to signal that God's *protection* over our physical life has been lifted, but God's *promise* for our future and His *presence* for our suffering remain intact. What if all three supports are removed at once? We are driven to the bare ground of our faith where only trusting love can hold us.

The Book of Job is known for its monumental affirmations of faith. With relative ease, we quote:

> . . . though He slay me, yet will I trust Him.
> . . . I know that my Redeemer lives,
> and
> . . . when He has tested me, I shall come forth
> as gold.
> (Job 13:15; 19:25; 23:10)

These statements are affirmations of trusting love. The depth of their meaning, however, can be understood only in the context from which they are spoken. In every case, the traditional supports for faith are removed so that Job's relationship with God is being tested at ground level.

When His Presence Seems Lifted

Preceding his declaration, "Though He slay me, yet will I trust Him . . . ," Job tells us he believes that God has lifted His hand of *protection* over his life. Because death is imminent, Job is willing to challenge God by defending the fact that he is innocent even though he suffers:

> Why do I take my flesh in my teeth,
> And put my life in my hands?
> (Job 13:14)

The answer is trusting love. In times of suffering, faith needs more than intellectual assent for the assurance that God is trustworthy. The experience of love in a personal relationship is the support base which holds up the reasoning of the mind and the commitment of the will. Therefore, we cannot isolate Job's affirmation of faith, "Though He slay me I will trust Him," from the attestation of love that lets Job take the risk, "Why do I take . . . my life in my hands?" Only trusting love can do that.

Yesterday I went to the hospital to minister to a faculty wife who had just received the news that her body had been invaded with inoperable cancer. As our eyes and hands met, she took charge of the conversation by saying, "This is the time that will test my faith. Can I apply to myself what I have said so often to others?" I could only nod as she went on to declare her trust in God and then to give thanks for a full and beautiful life. "My mother," she said, "died of cancer when I was fourteen. She never had the chance I have had to see my children grown with families of their own. So, I'll take it a day at a time and live every minute with thanksgiving."

I could only nod my head. She went on to tell of her witness to the attending nurse, her concern for her husband's health, and her interest in her family. As I left, I thanked her, "Jane, I came to minister to you, but you have ministered to me." Only then did she confess that she had cried out her tears before I came. Then, referring to the Book of Job which she and her husband had been studying, she smiled with the wryness of one who knows the truth and said, "Though He slay me, I will trust Him."

When His Promises Seem to Lapse

Job's second affirmation of faith is even more memorable than the first one. It has become the triumphant theme for Handel's *Messiah,* an aria which never fails to thrill us:

> For I know that my Redeemer lives,
> And He shall stand at last on the
>   earth;
> And after my skin is destroyed,
>   this I know,
> That in my flesh I shall see God.
> (Job 19:25–26)

Most of us, however, cannot fully appreciate the circumstances from which Job speaks. He has come to realize that God's *promise* for his future seems to be lost. Like us, his faith has been built upon the Word of God. In this case, it is not the written Word, but the spoken Word that has been communicated between friends. Job has learned to trust God's Word and knows that His *promises* for the future are assured. Like us in our healthy prosperity, Job lived with bright hope for the future. We learn this later on in the story when out of the depth of his suffering, Job recalls his days of peace and prosperity. He also remembers his confidence in God's *promises* for the future:

> Then I said, "I shall die in my nest,
> And multiply my days as the sand.
> My root is spread out to the waters,
> And the dew lies all night on my
>   branch.
> My glory is fresh within me,
> And my bow is renewed in my hand."
> (Job 29:18–20)

Job assumed that he had the *promise* of God for longevity, health, family, peace, prosperity, fame, and vitality. Now this *promise* appears to have failed. Job has lost all of his hope for the good things of life. What has happened to the *promises* of God? Job does not know. He can only hang on to the proof of the past when God's promises came true and the realities of the present in which he knows that he has not sinned.

> Oh, that my words were written!
> Oh, that they were inscribed in a book!
> That they were engraved on a rock
> With an iron pen and lead, forever!
> (Job 19:23–24)

This is a statement of trusting love that is almost beyond us. Job is saying that even though he will die, he is willing to have his words in a permanent record because the time will come when God will fulfill His *promise*. Think of it! Even though Job himself will never see God's *promise* fulfilled in his lifetime, he knows that God's Word is good. So good, in fact, that Job is then lifted in the Spirit to make a declaration of faith far, far beyond his time or knowledge:

> I know that my Redeemer lives,
> And He shall stand at last on the earth
> And after my skin is destroyed . . .
> That in my flesh I shall see God.
> (Job 19:25–26)

Believe it or not, against the apparent lapse of God's *promise* for Job's future, he actually foresees the Incarnation, the Resurrection, and his Redemption through Jesus Christ. Only trusting love can see that far.

My wife, Janet, and I have just returned from the funeral of her only brother who died unexpectedly at the age of sixty-seven. As I mentioned before, their ninety-two-year-old mother is in a nursing home, almost vegetating in a senile state. When my wife told her about the death of her only son, nothing registered. We began to debate the wisdom of taking her to the funeral, but decided the family needed her presence even if she did not know what was going on. Rain drenched the area the next day and we again debated the wisdom of taking her out and risking a cold. Something compelled us to stick with our earlier decision, so we bundled her up and took her to the funeral.

Entering a side door along a ramp for the handicapped,

we were surprised to be ushered directly into the funeral
parlor in full view of the mourners. Instantly, we saw on the
faces of the family the value of her being there and we heard
the audible gasp of surprise from our friends. For her, however, no sign of recognition let us know she was aware of
being at her son's funeral despite the flowers, open casket,
organ music, and tears. Watching her closely, I detected no
light of awareness in her eyes as the officiating minister read
the Scripture, gave the eulogy, and offered a homily of comfort for the family.

But then, to close the service, the pastor asked us to join
in the recitation of the Twenty-third Psalm which was printed
on the order of service. At the sound of the first word, "The
Lord is my shepherd . . . " a strong and firm voice began to
lead the congregation. It was Mom. Without missing a single
word, she led us through the Psalm. Awe swept over us as we
realized that Mom's lifetime of reading, memorizing, and
quoting the Word of God brought her back to reality and
became her *promise* when her only son died.

After dismissal, we took Mom forward to the casket.
Squinting to see his face, she asked, "Is this my boy?" Janet
answered, "Yes, it's Eldon." With full awareness now, Mom
asked her next question, "Did he make it to heaven?" Again,
Janet answered, "Yes, he's in heaven with Joyce and Daddy
now."

With that word of assurance, Mom lapsed back into the
fog of senility and rode home without another word. In her,
we saw trusting love at work. As with Job, God's *promise* had
been engraved on her heart and even after she had lost touch
with reality, it came back to her in the evidence that God had
answered her prayer and fulfilled His *promise*. Never again
will I assume that spiritual communication stops when it appears as if the mind is gone. Despite the suffering of senility,
a lifetime of love is holding Mom in communion with her
Lord.

When His Presence Seems Lost

Job's third affirmation of faith is made in the most difficult circumstances of all. Apparently, he has lost the *presence*

of God in his suffering. It is tough enough to stand physical suffering when God seems to lift His hand of *protection* from our lives or when His *promises* for the future seem to have lapsed, but to lose His *presence* is hell itself:

> Oh, that I knew where I might find
> Him,
> That I might come to His seat!
> > (Job 23:3)

> Look, I go forward,
> but He is not there,
> And backward,
> but I cannot perceive Him;
> When He works on the left hand,
> I cannot behold Him;
> When He turns to the right hand,
> I cannot see Him.
> > (Job 23:8–9)

God is gone. Like the spouse or friend who dies, the lonely survivor searches from room to room with the faint hope that death might have been only a bad dream. Instead, each line of search bumps against the harsh reality that the death is real and the person's presence is lost. Job goes through a similar process—searching backward and forward, right and left—only to encounter the personless places that had once been filled by the *presence* of God. He might have lost his faith in that moment. Instead, he gives us an affirmation for the ages:

> But He knows the way that I take;
> When He has tested me,
> I shall come forth as gold.
> > (Job 23:10)

Like Job's other affirmations of faith, this one does not stand alone. It echoes through the chambers of a universe where a suffering soul has searched for God and found only empty space. Yet, despite the emptiness, he declares that God is not dead and will reveal Himself once again. Only trusting love can hold in a time like that.

Earlier, I noted the text that I would choose if I had only

one sermon to preach. Now, I note the one sermon I would choose for suffering people to read. John Arthur Gossip tragically lost his wife and ministerial companion of many years. Although overwhelmed with grief, he insisted on preaching to his people as soon as possible. Returning to the pulpit, he announced the subject, "But When Life Tumbles In, What Then?" His text was Jeremiah 12:5:

> If you have run with the footmen,
>   and they have wearied you,
> Then how can you contend with
>   horses?
> And if in the land of peace,
> In which you trusted, they wearied you,
> Then how will you do in the flood plain
>   of the Jordan?

After confessing that he had been victimized by a fair-weather faith until his wife died, Dr. Gossip took his congregation with him through the verities of faith which are tested in death. In his conclusion, Gossip compares himself to Hopeful in *Pilgrim's Progress* as he speaks:

> For standing in the swelling of the Jordan, cold to the heart with its dreadful chill, and very conscious of the terror of its rushing, I too, like Hopeful, can call back to you who one day in your turn will have to cross it, "Be of good cheer, my brother, for I feel the bottom, and it is sound."[1]

Job gives the same message to all who suffer. Trusting love calls us back from the edge of death, the pit of despair, and the depths of loneliness:

> Be of good cheer, my brother, for I feel
> the bottom and it is sound.

We cannot forget that Job's relationship with God prefigures the love that binds Jesus with His Father. He, too, has His times for teasing, testing, and trusting God. The difference is that Job experiences the apparent loss of God's *protection, promise,* and *presence.* For Jesus, the loss is real. He dies alone and experiences hell. But today, thanks to the power of His Resurrection, for all who struggle with the apparent loss of God's *protection* for their lives, God's *promise* for their future, or God's *presence* for their suffering, Jesus is the One who speaks the ultimate affirmation of faith:

> Do not be afraid,
> I am the First and the Last.
> I am He who lives,
> and was dead, and behold,
> I am alive forevermore.
> (Rev. 1:17, 18)

Only love that holds can say that.

9
How Memory Heals

When we suffer and ask "Why?" we need memory for our healing. After a person has gone through the stages of denial, anger, negotiation, and acceptance of suffering, the next step is to gain the perspective of a new reality. As painful as it may be, perspective comes when we remember the days before our suffering. Memory is essential for our intellectual, emotional, and spiritual healing.

In his book, *Transitions: Making Sense of Life's Changes*, William Bridges envisions transformational change in the life of individuals or organizations as a drama in three acts.[1] Act I is entitled, "Old Endings," because we must let go of the unworkable elements of our past if we are to move forward into the future. Act II, then, is named "Transitions" because it takes time and trauma to rework our thinking when the old is ended and the new is not yet in place. Act III, however, becomes the story of "New Beginnings" in which hope is revitalized in the vision of a future that is even better than the past.

People who suffer because of a sudden change in their circumstances, whether it be disease, death, divorce, or displacement, become participants in the same drama. "Old Endings," "Transitions," and "New Beginnings" must be made in a succession of acts that will lead us to healing and hope.

After Job had worked through his rage in debate with his unsympathetic friends and reaffirmed his faith in a one-sided encounter with a silent God, neither he nor his friends had anything more to say to one another (Job 32:1). Job was left alone with his thoughts. Having been engaged in an exhausting emotional battle, he needed to climb above the conflict and see his suffering from the perspective of a new reality with which he must learn to live. As another attestation to the intellectual, emotional, and spiritual stature of the man, Job began the task of memory work—reviewing his theology, recalling his past, and rebuilding his identity.

Reviewing His Theology

Job's theology begins with a song. Bildad has just closed off all further conversation with one last cynical blast at all humankind:

> How much less man, who is a maggot,
> And a son of man, who is a worm?
> (Job 25:6)

This is more than Job can take. With equal impatience, he levels a parting shot at his friends-turned-enemies and gives up on them for good:

> How have you helped him who is
> without power?
> How have you saved the arm
> that has no strength?
> How have you counseled one
> who has no wisdom?
> And how have you declared sound
> advice to many?
> To whom have you uttered words?
> And whose spirit came from you?
> (Job 26:2–4)

Revealing, then, the difference between Bildad's bitter

spirit and his own persistent hope, Job breaks forth with one of the most majestic hymns of Scripture which extols the power of God over all creation, exalts the work of His Spirit, and concludes with the mystery of His grace:

> Indeed these are the mere edges
>   of His ways,
> And how small a whisper we hear
>   of Him!
> But the thunder of His power
>   who can understand?
>   (Job 26:14)

Whereas Bildad, from his peak of good health and prosperity, damns man, Job praises God from his valley of suffering and shame.

Advancing from his theology of God to his theology of man, Job acknowledges the sinfulness of human nature and the punishment of the wicked:

> This is the portion of a wicked man
>   with God,
> And the heritage of oppressors,
>   received from the Almighty.
>   (Job 27:13)

A litany of what has happened in Job's own life follows. The wicked will suffer the loss of children, possessions, health, peace, and respect (Job 27:14–23). Again, the contrast with Bildad's pessimism is obvious. Condemning man as a maggot, Bildad has betrayed the deficiency of his view of God. For Job, God is just; but for Bildad, God is brutal. Even more than that, Bildad has exposed the fact that he lacks a personal relationship with God based upon love and trust. If Bildad had been in Job's place, he would have cursed God and died long ago. Job, however, is realistic about the sinfulness of human nature and the wickedness of which we are capable. But this does not make man a maggot without mind or soul and worthy of being trampled underfoot. In direct refutation of such a cynical view, Job goes on to bring God and man together in a poetic discourse on wisdom:

Surely there is a mine for silver,
And a place where gold is refined.
Iron is taken from the earth,
And copper is smelted from ore.
Man puts an end to darkness,
And searches every recess
For ore in the darkness and the
    shadow of death.
He breaks open a shaft away from
    people . . . .
He puts his hand on the flint;
He overturns the mountains
    at the roots.
He cuts out channels in the rocks, . . .
He dams up streams from trickling; . . .

But where can wisdom be found?
And where is the place of
    understanding?
Man does not know its value,
Nor is it found in the land
    of the living . . . .

God understands its way,
And He knows its place . . . .
. . . He saw wisdom and declared it;
He prepared it,
    indeed, He searched it out.
            (Job 28:1–4, 9–11, 12–13, 23–27)

Job's understanding that we are created in the image of God is evident in the credit he gives to human achievements in the field of mining and metallurgy. Contemporary readers still marvel at his technological insights—far advanced for his time. He cites these achievements, however, for the purpose of drawing the limits of human ability to attain wisdom—the ability to see things whole—without a relationship with God based on reverential fear and discipline in righteousness. Not unexpectedly, Job pinches off the recall of his theological foundations with the capsule of his faith:

Behold, the fear of the Lord,
    that is wisdom.
And to depart from evil is
    understanding.
            (Job 28:28)

Throughout all the angry and accusatory interchange with his friends, Job has not wavered in his theological position. He still believes in the power of God, the punishment of the wicked, and the promise of wisdom. Having restated his position, however, he knows that he must go on. His theology does not answer the question, "Why do I suffer even though I have not sinned?" As part of his memory work, Job relives his quandary. He must hold on to the fundamentals of his faith at the same time that he must let go of the conclusion to which they have led him. The curtain falls on Act I, the drama of "Old Endings."

When we suffer, it is the time to ask ourselves, "What do I really believe about the character of God? What do I really believe about the nature of man?" and "What do I really believe about the relationship between God and man?" If we have positioned ourselves with Job rather than Bildad, we are ready to go on.

Remembering His Past

When we suffer, memory is one of the most effective agents for healing. Extensive studies of grieving people agree in their findings about the value of memory in mourning. Essentially, the past must be remembered in order to let it go. Therefore, when a loved one dies, counselors and friends do well to encourage the mourner to walk back through the memories of life with the deceased, whether those memories are good or bad. The same principle transfers to any kind of dramatic change in personal relationships which causes suffering—death, disease, divorce, or displacement. Remembering our past is the way in which we move through "Transitions," which is Act II in our drama of transformation.

Around our house we are learning the importance of memories in letting go. For the first time in thirty-five years, this fall our home became an "empty nest" when our fourth and youngest child enrolled at Seattle Pacific University, 2500 miles away. Initially, it seemed good not to stay awake and listen for his footsteps late at night or to pick up the

inevitable mess in his room. Then, one weekend, both my wife
and I became ill. Neither of us could admit the cause, except
that my wife is more honest about her feelings than I am. After
one violent sick spell, I heard her say, "He's gone forever." Her
exaggerated honesty made me realize that the "empty nest" is
a form of death itself which requires grief work.

Once the truth was out, we began to put together an
emotional scrapbook of our son's life with us—an inspiring
junior high school commencement address, a devastating tennis loss, a too-much, too-soon love affair, a blaring stereo, a
stupid fender-bender, a tennis idol for children, a supersensi-
tive spirit, and a life commitment at an altar of prayer.

True, he is gone forever in his dependence upon us—
but not in our gratitude for the years we had together. Our
memory work has served to set both him and us free to go
with hope into the future. Even now, we await his first return
for Christmas vacation with the light-hearted thought, *Only
Rob knows the secret of setting the digital clock in the car back
from daylight saving time.* We love him more now that we have
learned to let him go.

Job also engages in memory work as the bridge of transition between his old theology and his new reality. As a sure
sign of his good mental health, he speaks freely about the
grandeur of his past (Job 29). Of course, there is an air of
nostalgia in Job's memories, but not the kind that paralyzes
him. Remembering can become a fixation on gory details or
flights of fantasy created out of glossy generalities without a
balance of realism. Job is neither soggy nor sick as he remembers the glory of his past. He speaks in the past tense with
more gratitude than regret. He speaks of lost relationships,
not of lost things.

Remembering is the way in which we reveal our emotional attachments and our ego investment in those attachments. Noticeably and significantly, Job does not mention
either his wealth or his possessions in his memory work. As we
saw earlier, he held them loosely and with gratitude so that
when they were lost, he said:

> The Lord gave, and the Lord
>   has taken away;
> Blessed be the name of the Lord.
>   (Job 1:21)

As a true indication of the man, however, Job does not find it easy to give up his investment in interpersonal relationships. He remembers first his past relationship with God:

> Oh, that I were as in months past,
> As in the days when God watched over
> me;
> When His lamp shone upon my head,
> And when by His light I walked through
> darkness.
>
> (Job 29:2–3)

Almost in the same breath, Job links God's goodness with the memories of his family:

> Just as I was in the days of my prime,
> When the friendly counsel of God was
> over my tent;
> When the Almighty was yet with me,
> When my children were around me,
> When my steps were bathed with
> cream,
> And the rock poured out rivers
> of oil for me!
>
> (Job 29:4–6)

From here, Job's memory trail leads back to his former standing in his community:

> When I went out to the gate
> by the city,
> When I took my seat in the open
> square,
> The young men saw me and hid,
> The aged arose and stood;
> The princes refrained from talking; . . .
> The voice of nobles was hushed . . . .
>
> (Job 29:7–10)

Job, like us, is not without his vanity. A self-made man, he needs and loves the hush of awe with which young and old, princes and nobles alike, greeted him because of his wealth and power. But just as quickly as he recalls the honor given to him by the great and powerful, he makes it clear that he prefers to be remembered as the "father of the poor" (Job 29:16):

> .   delivering the poor who cry out,
> . . . saving the perishing man,
> . . . aiding the helpless widow,
> . . . serving as eyes for the blind,
> . . . becoming feet for the lame,
> . . . seeking the poor who have no voice,
>   and
> . . . rescuing the victims of oppression.
>   (Job 29:12–17)

Who can blame Job for his next thoughts? He remembers that he counted upon the goodness of God, the love of his family, the honor of his peers, and his championship of the poor to assure him long life, good health, and perpetual youth (Job 29:18–20). Job realizes that the connection between these emotional attachments of the past and his hope for the future has been severed. Undoubtedly, he had invested a large portion of himself in these relationships. Their loss meant that he had been stripped of the external support system for his identity and would have to rework the meaning of his life and reconstruct his sense of self-worth without them!

Job's wistful recognition of his lost relationships is like a parenthesis in his memory work. To make his emotional scrapbook complete, he returns to his remembering and draws out one more relationship which he loved—the power to lead and govern with wisdom and confidence:

> I chose the way for them,
>   and sat as chief;
> So I dwelt as a king in the army,
> As one who comforts mourners.
>   (Job 29:25)

By Job's example, we learn the rules for remembering when we suffer. Memory can implement our healing during the time of transition from "Old Endings" to "New Beginnings" if we:

    1. Keep our memories in the past tense.
    2. Keep our memories bright.
    3. Keep our memories balanced.

In contrast with Job's constructive remembering, some sufferers can never accept the new reality of their circumstances. They dwell on their suffering, romanticize their past, hold to their old attachments, and refuse to consider a future without full restoration of the days gone by. Of course, there is a fine line between faith that glorifies the past and faith that anticipates the future. Healing requires the willingness to remember the past with gratitude, but also to cut the emotional attachments to that past in order to move with hope into a new reality, whatever that may be.

The other day I heard a father say that he always referred to his dead son in the present tense. Whether in official or unofficial listings of his family, he said that the son is included among his brothers and sisters as if he were still living. At first I thought that these attempts to keep the spirit of his son alive were fitting expressions of a loving father. There is no doubt that his motive is good. But then I thought about the lesson from Job.

I wondered whether or not the father had ever been able to accept his son's death. Isn't there a connection between faith in God and the acknowledgment of our own mortality? Certainly, it did not appear as if his grief work had been done. Also, I wondered how his insistence on keeping his favorite son alive affected the other children in the family. In fairness to his faith and his family, he needs to acknowledge that his son is dead. As memory serves to recall the beauty of their relationship, he will be ready to move on to the new reality.

Job's memory work is not yet done. He must handle the discrepancy between his past glory and his present shame. On the same memory trail down which he came, Job reverses his thoughts with the words of a deep sigh, "But now . . ." (Job 30:1). Having completed the "Old Endings" of Act I, he must now proceed with added pain to draw the ludicrous contrast between his past and present condition:

> . . . his fame is mocked (30:1)
> . . . his honor is taunted (30:9)
> . . . his health is gone (30:16–19)

. . . his God is his enemy (30:20–23)
. . . his friends have failed him (30:24–29)

No more plaintive poetry can be found in Scripture or
human literature than Job's recognition of his new reality:

> I am a brother of jackals,
> And a companion of ostriches.
> My skin grows black
>   and falls from me;
> My bones burn with fever.
> My harp is turned to mourning,
> And my flute to the voice of those
>   who weep.
> (Job 30:29–31)

From the foundation of his theology, Job has begun to
build a bridge into the future by remembering the past with
gratitude, but leaving it behind by recognizing the new reality of his present condition. Now, in the next step toward
healing, he must rebuild his identity without the relational
attachments and emotional investments of the past. Reality
brings the curtain down on Act II.

Rebuilding His Identity

After reflecting upon his theological foundations, his
past glory and his present disgrace, Job is ready to begin
rebuilding his identity according to his new reality. All the
spiritual blessings and social supports upon which he previ-
ously depended for his identity have been stripped away. Fig-
uratively, at least, Job is naked before God and man. What's
left? As if already facing the Great Judgment, Job has nothing
left except the quality of his character. Here he is willing to
stand. Remembering now the covenant that he made with
God to keep himself "blameless and upright, fearing God and
shunning evil," Job proceeds with an accountability check on
his own character. Every possible sin of which he might be
accused is cataloged and Job declares not only his innocence,
but also his positive pursuit of righteousness.

Few of us would dare put our character on the line with the same declaration of independence from the sins of:

> . . . lust (31:1–4)
> . . . lying (31:5–8)
> . . . covetousness (31:9–12)
> . . . injustice (31:13–15)
> . . . lack of compassion (31:16–23)
> . . . idolatry (31:24–28)
> . . . vengeance (31:28–34)
> . . . waste of the land (31:38–40).

Like an attorney presenting his case before a cosmic court, Job exhausts every known charge that can be brought against him and then rests his case with the public challenge for anyone to speak now or forever hold his peace. More than that, at the gate of the city, in its marketplace, and through its streets, where the greatest man in the East has now become a byword, Job is willing to wear a placard on which his claims of innocence are written for all to see.

By this means, Job establishes his new identity. Admitting that all his past glory is gone and all his former social supports are lost, Job is literally stripped to the barest and innermost essentials of his character. He has nothing left but his integrity! By his declaration of innocence, Job is saying, "Even though all else is lost—my fame, fortune, family, and health—I have not lost my innocence. Remember me as a man of integrity."

Three times in my career stretching over twenty-six years as a college president, my integrity has been questioned by a colleague. In each case, the challengers were bright young people whom I had spotted as comers in their field and potential leaders in higher education. Without going into specifics, my words, my writing, and on one occasion, my business practices, were questioned. Each time, I had to search my conscience and review my conduct to determine whether or not I was guilty.

While recognizing that I might have been wiser in what I said and did, my self-conducted moral investigation revealed no motive, act, written word, or business transaction

that could not withstand public scrutiny or audit. In response
to the charges, then, I did not need position, power, privilege, or pity. People marveled at the nonretaliatory calm
with which I met the challenge. Assured that my integrity
was intact, I awoke one morning humming a song which
sprang from deep within my subconscious mind:

> Thou wilt keep him in perfect peace,
> Whose mind is stayed on thee,
> Through the sunshine and the shadows grim,
> He giveth perfect peace.

Job must have experienced the same kind of confidence.
Of course, his integrity test went far deeper and wider than
mine. My test was restricted to a narrow area of life and my
spiritual and social supports were still intact. Job's integrity
test was total. Mine was temporary as well. Job's new identity
as a man of integrity without divine blessing or human support appeared to be a permanent condition.

Critics are quick to charge Job with arrogance in his
claim of innocence. Not me. When Job announces, "Here is
my mark" (31:35), I hear the confidence of integrity, not the
trumpeting of self-righteousness. Certainly, we do not
charge Martin Luther with arrogance because he declared,
"Here I stand. So help me God, I can do no other." Integrity,
not arrogance, is speaking.

By remembering his past, Job has shown us how memory
heals during suffering. Restating our theological convictions, reliving our past glory, recognizing our current condition, and rebuilding our new identity is a process of healing
through suffering which causes us to change and grow.

The Ultimate Contradiction

Not by coincidence, we foresee the memory work of Jesus in Job's story. Time and time again, Jesus goes back to
remember His foundational convictions and His relationship
with His Father—Their oneness, Their love, and Their purpose. Yet, remembering for Jesus also included reflections on
past glory and recognition of His current circumstances. In

his letter to the Philippians, Paul draws the ultimate contradiction:

> . . . who, being in the form of God, did not
> consider it robbery to be equal with God,
>   but made Himself of no reputation,
> taking the form of a bondservant, and coming
> in the likeness of men,
>   And being found in appearance as a
> man, He humbled Himself, and became
> obedient to the point of death, even the
> death of the cross.
>   (Philippians 2:6–8)

Jesus, too, knew what it meant to be stripped of His past
glory with God and to lose the social supports for His identity.
His voluntary fall from glory to shame, throne to cross, King
to criminal, and life to death is the ultimate contradiction
which memory recalls. Isaiah's description of the "Suffering
Servant" is an unforgettable image because it is built of the
contrasts of memory which are so far apart that they seem
ludicrous. Such an image, however, is absolutely necessary if
we are to understand that Jesus had only His integrity to sustain Him during His trial, torture, humiliation, and death.

Going one ultimate step farther than Job, who could only
claim to be innocent of sin, but not without a sinful nature,
Jesus put out the public challenge, "Which of you convicts Me
of sin?" Silence followed and Jesus, like Job, rested His case.
Before His accusers, then, He stood silent. As docile as a lamb
going to the slaughter, Jesus was a man of integrity at peace
with Himself, His God and the whole world.

Job, too, falls silent as he rests his case. He has gone
through the living drama of transformation in which he has
cut off "Old Endings," worked through the trauma of
"Transitions," and initiated "New Beginnings" with integrity
as the mark of his new identity.

Memory has served Job well. He is on the way to healing from his doubts, bitterness, and regrets. He can do no
more for himself. Now Job needs someone to intervene who
can help his healing.

"Truly I am as your
spokesman before God!"
—Elihu

10
How Critics Help

When we suffer and ask "Why?" we need someone to
help us. Our first need is for a *comforter*—someone who loves
us, understands our pain and gives us the courage to go on.
Then we need a *counselor*—someone who listens to us, talks
to us, and leads us through our struggle with the question
"Why?" And, on occasion, we need a counselor who is a
critic—someone who still loves us, but dares to confront us
with the truth so that we will be open to hear God speak.
Even though the process is painful, critics who speak "the
truth in love" (Eph. 4:15) can help us.

Verbal violence has driven Job deeper and deeper into a
defensive position. To counter the hostility of his three
friends, he has not only built up a wall of self-protection for
his innocence but also launched an attack on God's justice
that borders on blasphemy. The culmination comes when Job
draws up a legalistic bill of particulars in which he defends
himself against every known sin and challenges anyone, including God, to find him guilty:

> Oh, that the Almighty
> would answer me,

> That my Prosecutor had written a
>   book!
> Surely I would carry it on my shoulder,
> And bind it on me like a crown;
> I would declare to Him the number
>   of my steps;
> *Like a prince I would approach Him.*
>   (Job 31:35–37, emphasis mine)

I admired Job until he spoke that last line. It is one thing for him to attest his innocence before God and man; it is quite another thing to swagger like a prince into the presence of God. Job comes dangerously close to assuming that his innocence makes him equal with God. Without question, in his efforts to justify himself before his friends and God, Job has built around himself an impregnable wall of defense. Even if God should speak, he could not hear Him!

The shock of suffering radicalizes our responses. Like Job, we cry out "Why?" in anger and despair. After these emotions subside, however, we see our suffering more objectively. But if we are in an environment where we have to defend ourselves as Job did, our responses become more and more radical. Violent action creates violent reaction. For instance, Job's three friends drive him to such rash and wordy statements in his own defense that they finally stop answering him. Likewise, Job's perception that God has become his silent, vengeful enemy causes him to attack his Friend and defend himself. So, whenever suffering is compounded by self-defense, there is the danger of taking a radical position as our point of no return. Our ego investment is too great.

Radical overcommitment is a danger whenever we invest ourselves in a cause. In our zeal to advance the cause, we are pushed farther and farther toward radical extremes until we cut off avenues for retreat or alternatives for change. During the tumultuous days of the early 1970s, I invited an outstanding Black professor to a teaching position at Seattle Pacific University. He met all the qualifications for the position—he had a contagious Christian testimony, an earned doctorate, and a reputation for masterful teaching. When the news of his pending appointment reached radical Black groups in the city, however, they pressured him to side with them. Consequently, he turned down the offer with the explanation that he could not be his own man in the political climate of the times. While not being an "Uncle Tom" by any measure, he refused to be pushed into a radical identity that would detract from his faith and his teaching. To be a Black professor in an urban Christian college in the early 1970s was a "lose-lose" situation.

The same hazard holds for any cause which we fully embrace. Over the years, I have witnessed the radicalization of people on both the right and the left who are forced into positions from which they have no retreat. Whether it is racism and feminism on the left or inerrancy and pro-life on the right, the danger of radical overcommitment persists. Even good causes with noble motives can degenerate into "lose-lose" situations.

Job came to this "dead end," not only with his three friends, but also with God. To swagger like a prince into the presence of God and dare Him to charge you with sin is more than radical overcommitment; it is insufferable arrogance. Job no longer needs a comforter or a counselor—he needs an objective critic to tell him the truth. Eliphaz, Bildad, and Zophar were right on one count—Job had become righteous in his own eyes (Job 32:1).

Enter Elihu, a young man who had witnessed the futile debate between Job and his friends and waited for his turn to speak. Elihu is angry—white hot with rage against both Job and his friends. Job aroused his wrath by trying to justify himself rather than God, but Eliphaz, Bildad, and Zophar equally raised his ire because they condemned Job without answer or cause. So, Elihu is cast into the role of a critic. In a succession of three speeches, he contradicts Job's argument, condemns his self-righteousness, and creates a climate in which God can speak. After each speech, he invites Job to answer him.

It is Job's turn to be silent. His defenses crumble as he hears an angry young man speak the truth with love and the "breath of the Almighty." Thanks to Elihu his critic, Job steps back from his argument, sees that he is wrong, and submits himself to the silence in which God can speak. Critics can help us by refuting our closed position, recommending creative options, and readying us for God's revelation.

Refuting Our Closed Position

Critics can save or destroy us. Emerson called the critic an ". . . unpaid guardian of our souls." Another person, however, said of a critic, "I didn't think he touched me until I tried to shake my head." All of us know what he meant. We usually think of our critics as persons who "get an edge in wordwise" and lop off our heads.

According to Emerson's definition, Elihu qualifies as a critic. He serves as the "unpaid guardian" of Job's soul. How could this be when he is introduced as being so angry with Job? What is the difference between his anger and the rage of Job's other three friends? In his own words, Elihu defines the difference. He is angry—so much so that he says his words are about to burst out of his belly ". . . like wine that has no vent . . ." (Job 32:19).

There is a time for anger. In his book, *Creative Suffering*, Paul Tournier devotes a full chapter to this subject. He notes, "Anger and acceptance are contradictory in theory, but in practice they hold hands like the dancers in a folk dance."[1] To illustrate his point, Tournier repeats the story of an old Italian man who has been victimized time and time again by the cruelties of life. His loneliness is compounded by a language barrier. No one understands him; no one accepts him. Didier Duruz, a psychiatrist, hears his sad story, becomes angry for him and pounds the table muttering the words, "It's not fair. It's not fair." Tournier reports that the old man's eyes light up as he realizes that someone understands and accepts him for the first time.[2]

Elihu's anger does not alienate Job. In fact, his show of rage probably comes as welcome relief from the vague attempts of his three friends to remain cool, calm, and collected when their insides bubbled and boiled with anger. But make no mistake, the expression of anger may be no better than the repression of anger. Catharsis or "cleaning out" may be therapeutic for the angry person, but it often leaves the victims of rage in shambles.

A person I know has a reputation for a hair-trigger temper. At the slightest provocation, he bursts upon people, vents his anger, and leaves his victims limp. Moments later, he

nonchalantly returns as if nothing happened. The truth is
that his anger is a weapon of intimidation used to demand his
own way. Something more is required for expressive anger to
dance hand-in-hand with honest acceptance of people.

In his own words, Elihu tells us how his anger will be
tempered. He begins by claiming to speak with the *"breath
of the Almighty"* (32:8). His choice of words to describe
the "Spirit" within him is not accidental. The "breath of the
Almighty" of which Elihu speaks is the same Spirit that
breathes life into all of God's works—Creation, Incarnation,
Resurrection, and Revelation. Notably, neither Job nor his
friends ever made the same claim for any of their wordy
speeches. To be sure, Elihu's claim is bold. Yet, as we follow
his speeches, the evidence is on his side. He is a critic who
speaks with the understanding of the Spirit of God.

As another check-and-balance on his anger, Elihu tells
Job that he will speak with *impartiality.* During their debate, Job and his friends had chosen sides and pushed their
arguments to radical extremes. Emotions ran so high that
anyone who entered the debate would be pressed to take one
side or the other. Elihu, however, prays that he might be
freed from bias in his response:

> Let me not, I pray,
>   show partiality to anyone;
> Nor let me flatter any man.
> For I do not know how to flatter,
> Else my Maker would soon take me
>   away.
>
> (Job 32:21–22)

In this prayer, we see another reason Elihu qualifies as a
critic. His claim to impartiality is linked to his sense of responsibility to God. Only a person who has the mind of God's
Spirit can speak this way. Elihu is not bragging about his skills
in impartial debate; he is acknowledging his responsibility
before God to speak without bias.

Impartiality can be cold and unfeeling, but Elihu claims
another dimension of the Spirit that assures Job of fairness.
Just before Elihu tells Job that he is wrong to assume he is
pure and God is unjust, he *identifies* with him as a fallible
human being:

> I also have been formed out of clay.
> Surely no fear of me will terrify you,
> Nor will my hand be heavy on you.
> (Job 33:6b–7)

What a contrast with the attitude of Eliphaz, Bildad, and Zophar! They assumed that they were superior to Job and argued from their lofty positions. Elihu, however, comes down to Job's level with compassion for his suffering, his shame, and even his rantings against God. Now we know why Job fought so ferociously with his wise and elderly friends but now is willing to listen to a brash and angry young man. He knows Elihu means it when he says that he identifies with him as a fallible human being. When genuine compassion is the attitude communicated by our critics, we will hear them out even though it hurts.

For any of us who are called to be critics for our friends in times of suffering, Elihu sets the standard. Only as we have the mind of the Spirit of God can we speak. But how will we know when we have His mind? A check-and-balance system is the answer. We will become emotionally involved with the person so that he or she will know of our acceptance, even if we are angry. We will speak impartially as the Spirit reminds us of our responsibility before God when we deal with the dignity, freedom, and future of another person whom He has created and whom He loves. And we will be able to identify with the suffering of that person because we too are fallible and finite human beings. Thus, in the critical balance of the Holy Spirit, we are qualified as critics when we are involved with the person, inspired by the Spirit, impartial in our argument, and identified with his humanity. Then, and only then, do we dare say to a suffering soul who needs correction:

> Truly I am as your spokesman before
> God.
>
> (Job 33:6)

Many of us are willing to be God's spokesmen, but few of us are willing to accept the conditions. Yet, if we speak as critics without the mind of the Spirit, we compound the suffering of the person even if we speak the truth. Still worse, we fail to help the sufferer struggle with the question "Why?" on the way to healing. Job needs Elihu to refute the radical position he has taken on his own innocence and God's injustice. He will hear him because his attitude confirms his claim that he speaks with the "breath of the Almighty."

Recommending Creative Options

You have to be creative to survive around our house. Four children know how to search for creative options when it appears that we have come to a dead end. Not long ago, the whole family circled together at our round table in the kitchen and began to recall their life with Mom and Dad. One said, "I remember Mom fixing a big dinner and then trying to slow us down by saying, 'Let's all relax and enjoy ourselves.'" Another asked, "What about Dad?" "Oh, that's easy," our youngest son answered. "He always says to us, 'Let's look at the options.'" Creativity is the ability to look at the options when arguments are stalemated or decision-making is frustrated.

Elihu confronts Job with the fact that his radical claims for his own innocence and God's apparent injustice have brought him to a dead end.

> Surely you have spoken in my hearing,
> And I have heard the sound of your
>   words, saying,
> "I am pure, without transgression;
> I am innocent,
>   and there is no iniquity in me.
> Yet He finds occasions against me,
> He counts me as His enemy;
> He puts my feet in the stocks,
> He watches all my paths."
>   (Job 33:8–11)

Wasting no words, Elihu refutes Job's position with surgical precision:

> Look, in this you are not righteous.
> I will answer you,
> For God is greater than man.
>   (Job 33:12)

At this critical juncture, Elihu's sensitivity to Job's condition takes over. Avoiding the tactics of Eliphaz, Bildad, and Zophar, he does not immediately pursue the argument that will condemn Job and justify God. Rather, he suggests that Job look at some options not yet considered. The first option is this: God may be speaking to him in ways Job has not heard because he has insisted that God speak only one way—directly to him. Elihu reminds him of this alternative:

> For God may speak in one way,
>   or in another,
> Yet man does not perceive it.
> In a dream, in a vision of the night, . . .
> Then He opens the ears of men,
> And seals their instruction.
> (Job 33:14–16)

Job is not alone in his selective deafness. Each of us brings a bias to our listening for the voice of God. For Job, a left-brained man of logical analysis, it is evidently a bias against the intuitions of the right-brain through which God also speaks. In fact, with just a touch of satire, Elihu suggests that God can speak through a vision in the night like the one which Eliphaz cited as the authority for his word of wisdom. By rejecting Eliphaz's argument, Job had also rejected a means of communication through which God may speak.

I am the first to confess my selective deafness in listening for the voice of God. I too am trained as a left-brained person who relies upon logical analysis for decision-making. My bias is aggravated by the fact that I grew up in a church where emotion overruled reason. Reacting against that background, I find it hard to hear the intuitive words of knowledge and prophecy that my charismatic friends speak of as the voice of God. My hearing is further hindered when a person speaks about a vision from God which reveals new truth or foretells the future.

When a long-time friend went on national television to tell of a vision from God with the promise of a great revival, my skepticism turned him off. Later, when his prediction did not come true with evidence as visible as his vision, my bias received reinforcement. At that moment, I needed Elihu to say to me, ". . . God may speak in one way, or in another . . . in a dream, in a vision of the night." Who am I to demand that God speak my way? According to Scripture, I must test the spirits, but with an open rather than a closed mind. Like Job, I must consider the option of intuition as a means of God's instruction (Job 33:16).

Through the mind of the Spirit, Elihu has another option Job has not considered as a reason for his suffering. It is to reveal the promise of God's grace as seen from the depth of suffering when death is near:

> If there is a messenger for him,
> A mediator, one among a thousand,
> To show man His uprightness,
> Then He is gracious to him, and says,
> "Deliver him from going down
>   to the Pit;
> I have found a ransom."
> (Job 33:23–24)

All the elements of redemption through Jesus Christ are contained in this sentence. He will come as the Mediator for those who suffer, the Ransom for those who sin, and the Deliverer for those who die. Job has built his case on the justice of God; Elihu reminds him that he has forgotten the grace of God. Through grace, Job is promised the return of his youthful joy (33:25), the restoration of his righteousness (33:26), and the redemption of his soul (33:28).

Grace has still another quality which Job has forgotten in his attack on the character of God. Elihu reminds him that God's justice does not work like a "cash register" in which sin is automatically punched in and punishment is instantly rung up. Through grace, God's patience intervenes between sin and punishment to woo and win us with His love:

> Behold, God works all these things,
> Twice, in fact, three times with a man,
> To bring back his soul from the Pit,
> That he might be enlightened with the
>   light of life.
> (Job 33:29–30)

On the keynote of grace, Elihu stops and invites Job to answer him. For the first time, this wise and righteous man is silent. Perhaps he is pondering the options that Elihu has presented. More likely, though, he realizes that God is speaking through Elihu and in His presence he is in "awe"—a biblical word of reverence that means, "I shut my mouth."

Refuting False Arguments

By showing an attitude of acceptance and creating a climate of teaching, Elihu has earned the right to refute Job's errors in his argument. At this point, many scholars disagree with Elihu. Because he appears to repeat the same tedious arguments advanced by Eliphaz, Bildad, and Zophar in defense of God's justice and against Job's righteousness, these scholars conclude that he has no relevant role in the Book of Job. If Elihu's contentions (chapters 34 and 35) are read as sterile theology, the critical scholars are right. Elihu sounds just like Eliphaz, Bildad, and Zophar. But if the same arguments are read in the personalized context of Elihu's genuine concern for Job, they are indispensable to the Book.

Job's case is built on the foundation of his innocence. In his zeal to prove his case, he strikes out against the justice of God because he is treated no better than the wicked who deserve to suffer. Elihu divides the case into two parts. First, he deals with Job's thinly veiled charge that God is unjust. Like Eliphaz, Bildad, and Zophar, he quotes Job's position verbatim:

> For Job has said, "I am righteous,
> But God has taken away my justice;
> Should I lie concerning my right?
> My wound is incurable,
>   though I am without transgression."
> (Job 34:5–6)

Beware of critics who use quotes from the person whom they criticize. More often than not, either the words are twisted, the inflections are changed, or the context is forgotten. When this happens, antagonism between the contending parties is aggravated over the issue of accuracy. Communication breaks down and any hope of dealing with substance is lost. Communication theory, therefore, stresses the principle of qualifying quotations with the preface, "I think I heard you say . . . ." rather than bluntly stating, "You said . . . ." Elihu is not that gentle. Either as a credit to his listening during the long debate or to the climate of confidence that he created in the introduction to his speech, Elihu quotes Job and Job does not protest.

Elihu then goes for the jugular vein of Job's complaint. Although refusing to curse God and die, Job has teetered on the brink of blasphemy by implying the conclusion:

> It profits a man nothing
> That he should delight in God.
> (Job 34:9)

The words sound familiar. Satan himself is the one who first snarled, "Does Job serve God for nought?" (Job 1:9). His question not only impugns the righteousness of Job but also demeans the character of God. For Job, it means that he is righteous only because God prospers him. For God, it means that He plays favorites. This is why Elihu is angry. Job has come within a hair's-breadth of proving Satan right. To preserve his own righteousness, he has attacked the justice of God.

Elihu fights fire with fire. In a no-nonsense discourse, he defends the character of a just God and appears to confirm the position taken by Eliphaz, Bildad, and Zophar:

> Therefore listen to me,
>   you men of understanding:
> Far be it from God to do wickedness,
> And from the Almighty to commit
>   iniquity.
> For He repays man according to His
>   work,
> And makes man to find a reward
>   according to his way.
> (Job 34:10–11)

Truth is truth. Elihu actually repeats the arguments of Job's three friends in his defense of the justice of God. They too spoke the truth, but with the wrong attitude. Job also spoke this truth, but came to the wrong conclusion. In trying to deal with the contradiction of suffering even though he was innocent, Job chose to justify himself at the expense of God's character. Therefore, Elihu lays a charge on Job that is just as heavy, if not heavier, than the condemnation of Eliphaz, Bildad, and Zophar:

> "Job speaks without knowledge,
> His words are without wisdom."
> Oh, that Job were tried to the utmost,
> Because His answers are like those of
>   wicked men!
> For he adds rebellion to his sin;
> He claps his hands among us,
> And multiplies his words against God.
> (Job 34:35–37)

Once again, Elihu pauses and waits for Job to answer. Similar words had inflamed him when they were spoken by his three friends. But no answer comes. Job's silence is consent. He knows that Elihu speaks the truth with the "breath of the Almighty" in a climate of care—and with a tone of teaching. His critic is his help.

Job's case against God has another side. Not only has he questioned the justice of God; but he has justified himself. So, Elihu takes on the task of telling Job the truth for the second time by pointedly refuting the folly of Job's self-righteousness. Yet this time he is more cautious about starting his argument by quoting Job. Instead, he asks him a question that leads to a quotation:

> Do you think this is right?
> Do you say,
> "My righteousness is more than God's"?
> For you say,
> "What advantage will it be to You?
> What profit shall I have,
>   more than if I had sinned?"
> (Job 35:2–3)

Of course, Job would deny that his righteousness is more than God's. Eliphaz, Bildad, and Zophar had accused him of the same folly, but with their own self-justifying intent. Elihu, however, is able to objectify the issue by asking a probing question rather than making a damning declaration. So, for the first time, Job hears Elihu and understands the implications of his self-righteous position. He also hears himself violating his better judgment when he whines, "What profit shall I have, more than if I had sinned?"

We can't be too hard on Job. If we are honest, we will confess that we have asked the same question. Remember the man who questioned the justice of God because thieves had stolen his wife's jewels? He complained, "I work hard and try to live a good life . . . and then this happens." Somewhere in the life history of anyone who suffers, the same question is asked, "Why try to live righteously and still suffer?" Deep in our thoughts is the idea that sinners have more fun even though they will have to pay for it in the long run. If Satan has a favorite trap, this is it. Once he gets us to link righteousness with prosperity, he sets us up for disillusionment through suffering.

Elihu's answer to Job's questions is to ask other questions:

> If you sin,
>   what do you accomplish against Him?
> Or, if your transgressions are
>   multiplied, what do you do to Him?
> If you are righteous,
>   what do you give Him?
> Or what does He receive from your hand?
>   (Job 35:6–8)

Job knows the answer. His sin or righteousness has no effect upon the character of God. He remains pure and holy no matter what human beings do. Our sin or righteousness, therefore, affects only the quality of our character and that of our culture. Intellectually, Job knew this truth, but he had refused to accept it emotionally. God is neither seduced nor blackmailed by our righteousness.

Elihu has still more to say about Job's self-righteousness. Along with all who suffer and are oppressed, Job wants relief by the power of God more than he wants reconciliation in the presence of God. In one of the most often-quoted passages in the Book of Job, Elihu puts his self-righteous friend in the company of all who suffer by asking a poignant question:

> Because of the multitude of
>   oppressions they cry out;
> They cry out for help because of the
>   arm of the mighty.
> But no one says,
>   "Where is God my Maker,
> Who gives songs in the night,
> Who teaches us more
>   than the beasts of the earth,
> And makes us wiser
>   than the birds of heaven?"
>   (Job 35:9–11)

In a word, Elihu is telling Job that God will not answer him as long as his pride stands in the way. Furthermore, Elihu reminds him that it is the height of folly for Job to assume he is justified because God has neither answered his demands nor punished him for his sins. The final indictment is severe.

> . . . Job opens his mouth in vain;
> He multiplies words without
>   knowledge.
>   (Job 35:16)

It is quiet time again. Elihu pauses for Job's answer. Without question, the truth has stung him. To hear his own rash words and radical conclusions repeated by another voice helps him realize the error of his folly.

Elihu's tactic has continuing value. When I began my training as a hospital chaplain, the instructor insisted that his students preface their response to patients with the words "You feel . . . ." Not only did he want to teach us sensitivity to the patient's feelings, but he also wanted the patient to hear his or her own words of feeling, whether positive or negative. Presumably, this process encouraged the patient to work through the pain of negative feelings and then turn toward the healing of positive affirmation. Later, we learned that the theological faultline lay in the assumption that self-healing is possible through this process without the resources of God's redemption.

Job needs more than the refutation of his self-righteousness. His silence is its own testimony. His head is bowed in shame and he is burdened with guilt. Elihu realizes what the truth has done to Job and he knows that he cannot leave him in despair. So, as further proof that he speaks with the "breath of the Almighty," Elihu shifts from critic to comforter. He balances out his scathing indictments with the assurance that God is good and great.

Readying God's Entrance

Youthful critics sometimes forget that they have a responsibility for presenting constructive solutions to the problems they expose. During the rash and wordy years of the student protest during the late 1960s and early 1970s, campus newspapers were filled with caustic criticism of institutions and their leaders. Presidents' offices were trashed and their occupants driven to resignation. Time and time again, I met with campus leaders and newspaper editors to ask, "What constructive solutions do you have for the problems against which you protest?" Answers to the question usually came "off the wall" or fell into the category of shifting responsibility back to the administration. Especially in newspaper editorials, I responded to the writers by reminding them that freedom of the press includes responsibility for both critical comments and constructive solutions. In most cases, the message never got through. The fact that campus radicals either burned out early or joined the Establishment tends to prove they had no agenda beyond protest and criticism.

As conclusive proof that Elihu has the mind of the Spirit of God, his speeches move from refuting Job's self-righteousness to reminding his friend of God's goodness and greatness. In other words, he proposes a constructive solution for the critical indictment he has leveled against Job. The solution resides in the character of God. *He is good:*

> Behold, God is mighty,
>   but despises no one;
> He is mighty in strength of
>   understanding.

> He does not preserve the life
> of the wicked,
> But gives justice to the oppressed.
> (Job 36:5-6)

Elihu is assuring Job that God's justice is tempered with
mercy. Urgently, then, he pleads with Job to give up his
attacks on the justice of God and turn away from the attitude
of self-righteousness. Not by coincidence, Elihu avoids the
word "repent" which Eliphaz, Bildad, and Zophar had used
as a weapon against Job. Instead, he urges him to choose
affliction rather than iniquity if given no other choice (Job
36:21).

Elihu's words now take on wings. As he reflects on the
goodness of God, he begins to sing:

> Remember to magnify His work,
> Of which men have sung.
> (Job 36:24)

Nature joins him on the chorus. In the distance, he sees
a rising storm with the rhythm of its rain and the thunder of
its voice:

> Indeed, can anyone understand the
> spreading of clouds,
> The thunder from His canopy?
> (Job 36:29)

His question prompts a powerful hymn to the greatness
and the glory of God (37:1-13). In the elements of nature—
thunder, rain, snow, ice, wind, and whirlwind—Elihu sees
the hand of God at work bringing about His great and good
purpose on earth:

> He causes it to come,
> Whether for correction,
> Or for His land,
> Or for mercy.
> (Job 37:13)

God is not whimsical in the exercise of His power. He
always has a purpose that is good—to correct us, to feed us,

or to love us. As Elihu has spoken with the "breath of the Almighty," he sings with the Spirit of understanding.

Turning to Job with his new note of hope, Elihu says:

> Listen to this, O Job;
> Stand still and consider the wondrous
> works of God.
> Do you know when God dispatches
> them,
> And causes the light of His cloud
> to shine?
> Do you know how the clouds are balanced,
> Those wondrous works of Him
> who is perfect in knowledge?
> (Job 37:14–16)

With this open question, Job is ready to hear the voice of God. Then, as quickly as the storm arose, it passes. The earth is silent, the air is clear, the sky is golden, and the stage is set for God to speak. Elihu has served the Spirit well. Beginning as an angry critic with the aim of defending the justice of God and condemning the self-righteousness of Job, he ends with a hymn of praise to the goodness and the glory of God— with Job standing still and ready to listen for the first time.

Stepping Aside for God

Think of Elihu as a forerunner who prepares the way for the coming of God. In this role he stands parallel with much of the prophetic tradition of John the Baptist. Both are remembered as angry young men who preached justice and repentance for a short time and then disappeared from the scene. Yet, the significance of their ministry draws the highest commendation from God. John the Baptist had the privilege of introducing Jesus to the world and baptizing Him with the seal of God's voice saying, "This is my beloved Son in whom I am well-pleased." Then, with an uncanny sense of spiritual timing, John stepped aside with the joy of knowing that Jesus would increase as he decreased. Elihu plays a similar role in the spiritual drama of Job. He sets the stage for God to speak and introduces Him through the voice of thunder. But then without the drama of John's violent death, Elihu simply disappears from the scene. Yet, he receives the highest commendation of a prophet and a pastor when God begins to speak out of the whirlwind. There is no break between his voice and the voice of God. Like John the Baptist, Elihu decreases and God increases. He is our example of a critic who helps us.

"Now prepare yourself
like a man; I will question
you and you will answer Me."
—God

11

How God Speaks

When we suffer and ask "Why?" nothing is settled until God speaks. Otherwise, the question "Why?" hangs over our heads like the sword of Damocles. Our human nature demands an answer but unless God speaks, we will choose the answer of a blasphemer, an atheist, or a fatalist. A blasphemer curses God at the risk of death. An atheist denies God at the expense of meaning. A fatalist gives up on God at the price of freedom.

Job refuses to curse, deny, or give up on his God. As impatient as his suffering has made him, he still awaits God's Word. As arrogant as his righteousness has made him, he remains open to the voice of God. Patience is a virtue tested and nurtured in suffering. With our current emphasis upon the instant remedy and the quick fix, we do not learn patience. We pray on the run and demand an immediate answer. In his Epistle, James reminds us of what we lose. Using Job as his example, he writes about the blessing of perseverance:

> Indeed we count them blessed who
> endure. You have heard of the

132

> perseverance of Job and seen the
> end intended by the Lord—that the
> Lord is very compassionate and merciful.
> (James 5:11)

Job's perseverance is blessed by God's compassion and mercy. The connection is not coincidental. God may answer our impatient prayers and arrogant demands, but if He does, we never learn the meaning of the fullness of His compassion and mercy.

Sometimes it takes suffering to slow us down. At least for a period of time, even the behavior pattern of a Type "A" personality is altered. According to Friedman and Rosenman in their book *Type "A" Behavior and Your Heart,* the Type "A" person is ". . . aggressively involved in a chronic, incessant struggle to achieve more and more in less and less time, and if required to do so, against the opposing efforts of other things and persons."[1] When I looked up this book in my personal library to find the definition of Type "A" behavior, I realized that my lifestyle is becoming more and more dictated by the "hurry sickness." Then, when I turned to the front page to get the bibliographical data on the book, I was greeted by a note from the friend who had sent it to me. He is the highly successful and socially prominent chairman of the board of an international corporation whose energy level suddenly faded. He ended up in the hospital for triple-bypass surgery on the cholesterol-clogged arteries of his heart. From his bed during convalescence, he sent the book to me with this note on the flyleaf:

> To: my good friend, David McKenna
>   —easy reading, yet something to think
>   about for future good health and
>   vitality.
>   Your Friend in Christ,
>   Chuck
>   Another Type "A"

His veiled warning scared me, but his recommendation of the book as ". . . something to think about . . . ." showed me how suffering had slowed him down to thoughtful reflection. I had known Chuck only as a man in a hurry, but then I remembered that the next time I met him after his recovery, he was full of gratitude and praise to God. The patience of suffering is far more than gritty endurance; it can be the opportunity to reflect upon the fullness of God's compassion and mercy.

Job still must learn that he cannot dictate the way in which God speaks. He demanded a courtroom setting with a legal contest over his innocence. Instead he gets a whirlwind in the desert with God asking the questions:

> Who is this who darkens counsel
> By words without knowledge?
> Now prepare yourself like a man;
> I will question you,
>   and you shall answer Me.
>   (Job 38:2–3)

God finally grants Job his request for an audience. He meets him where he is and speaks to him on the level of his understanding. He even accepts Job's challenge for a contest of questions and answers. But to Job's surprise, He gives no answers; He only asks questions.

God Speaks to Our Dignity

God is a master teacher. At the same time that He accepts Job's challenge for a battle of wits, He uses the question as His teaching tool. What a compliment to the intelligence of Job! God might have crushed him under the power of His omniscience, but instead He honors his intellectual capacity by stretching Job's mind to think about questions that he had failed to consider in his rantings about his innocence and God's injustice. What an insight into the character of God! He will never violate the freedom and the dignity of His human creation. As always, He comes to us first with a question, not an answer. Like a master teacher, God knows that the spiritual insights we gain for ourselves are the elements of wisdom and redemption.

Job demands an immediate audience with God; he learns to wait. He insists upon a definitive answer from God; Job gets only another question. He poses a legal and ethical question to God; he faces a spiritual and moral issue. At this point we find ourselves at the very heart of the message of the Book of Job. Job demands an answer to his questions, "Why me? Why this? Why now?" God ignores these questions. Instead, he asks Job, "Who am I?" and "Who are you?" The fundamental truth is this: When we ask, *"Why must I suffer?"* God answers, *"Who am I?"*

God Speaks to Our Doubt

God has good reason for not responding directly to Job's question, "Why do I suffer?" It appears as if Job is asking about the justice of God. But God knows what is in Job's heart. Out of the depths of his suffering, he has doubts about the greatness of God. Anyone who suffers knows what Job's hidden question is: *Does God really know what He is doing?* Those of us who have had to live with the suffering of an innocent person have asked the same question.

Not long ago, a friend of mine died. His two-year-old daughter had preceded him in death by forty-five years. A beautiful, blonde child, she was stricken overnight by acute leukemia and died within hours. When her father died forty-five years later, his son opened the lock box that contained his private papers. Everything was in order—his will, his insurance, his bonds, and his bank accounts. No paper was out of place. Therefore, the newspaper clipping that rested on the top of all his other precious papers told its own story. It was the obituary of his first and only daughter who had died at the age of two! To the day of his death he apparently kept asking, "Does God really know what He is doing?"

Honesty requires each of us to confess that we have asked the same question about God. Few of us would dare speak it openly. But all of us have had its edge of doubt penetrate our faith. From a human standpoint, my greatest moment of glory came when I became a finalist for the position as Secretary of Education in President Reagan's Cabinet, as I've already mentioned. At the last moment, however, political winds shifted and another person got the appointment. My wife and I were stunned because we thought we had prayed through to the assurance that the position would be ours. Although openly we accepted the disappointment as God's will, secretly we asked, "Does God know what He is doing?" Why would He lead us to the brink of glory and then let our hopes be smashed to the ground?

The good theology of a Peanuts cartoon rescued me. Woodstock, the wee yellow bird, is shown flying blissfully toward what appears to be an open window. Instead of flying into the house, he crashes at breakneck speed into a clear pane of glass and flutters to the ground. Shaking his head and staggering to his feet, Woodstock begins kicking at the corner of the house. Linus, who has witnessed the whole scene, comes along and offers this advice, "Don't blame the house just because you tried to fly through a closed window."

Hindsight tells me that my aspirations for a national position blinded me to the fact that I too was trying to fly through a closed window. Out of my own frustrated ambition, I blamed God for my disappointment. Although the event is now history, I must confess there are still times when I reflect upon that lost moment and wonder, "Did God really know what He was doing?"

Whatever the motivation behind Job's implied question of doubt, God answers him with a fusillade of questions which Job cannot answer. First, God asks, *Do you know how I created the universe?* Using architectural terms that Job can understand, God begins at the beginning:

> Where were you when I laid the
>   foundations of the earth?
> Tell Me, if you have understanding.
> Who determined its measurements?
> Surely you know!
> Or who stretched the line upon it?
> To what were its foundations fastened?
> Or who laid its cornerstone,
> When the morning stars sang together,
> And all the sons of God shouted for
>   joy?
>
> (Job 38:4–7)

God might have rested His case on *creation ex nihilo.* Instead, He presses on to ask Job if he understands the elements He used to build the universe:

> . . . who shut in the *sea* with doors . . . ?
> (38:8)
> . . . Have you commanded the *morning*
>   since your days began . . . ?
> (38:12)
> . . . Have you entered the *springs*
>   *of the sea?*
> (38:16)
> . . . Where is the way to the *dwelling*
>   *of light?*
> And *darkness*, where is its place?
> (38:19)

No doubt remains. To create the world out of nothing is a mystery that will forever confound the human mind. Scientists have been able to put a giant telescope the size of a schoolbus into outer space with the hope of seeing to the edge of the universe and perhaps explaining its origin. They will continue to be confounded because human intelligence cannot comprehend eternity. One honest scientist put it wisely when asked to describe in 150 words or less his research into the nature of the universe. He wrote "I don't know" fifty times.

God poses another question for Job, *"Do you know how I control My creation?"* From the basic elements required for the creation and construction of the earth, God turns to questions about environmental control—snow, hail, wind, floodtide, thunderbolt, wilderness, rain, dew, ice, and frost. Again, despite all our scientific advancements in environmental control, the weather remains unmanageable and unpredictable. A panel of economic experts spent an hour discussing the future of our world economy. At the close of the discussion, the moderator asked them if they knew of one element on which the world economy turned. With one voice, they answered, "The weather."

In further response to His own question, "Do you know how I control My creation?" God goes on to challenge Job on the *mysteries of outer space:*

> Can you bind the cluster of the
>   Pleiades,
> Or loose the belt of Orion?
> Can you bring out Mazzaroth
>   in its season?

> Or can you guide the Great Bear
> with its cubs?
> Do you know the ordinances
> of the heavens?
> Can you set their dominion
> over the earth?
> (Job 38:31–33)

Returning once again to His control of the weather, God adds the *dimension of wisdom* to the questions of power and understanding. He reminds Job that it is one thing to have power over all creation and understanding of its mysteries, but it is quite another thing to have the wisdom to run it:

> Who can number the clouds by
> wisdom?
> Or who can pour out the bottles
> of heaven,
> When the dust hardens in clumps,
> And the clods cling together?
> (Job 38:37–38)

God has proven His point again. His power, understanding, and wisdom for the creation and control of the universe are proof that He knows what He is doing. But there is more. God's creation includes living beings as well as energy, matter, time, and space. Thus, He also asks Job, *"Do you know how I care for My creation?"*

Like the processional leading into Noah's ark, God parades the animals of His creation before the mind's eye of Job—lions, ravens, mountain goats, deer, donkeys, onagers, oxen, ostriches, horses, hawks, and eagles (Job 38:39–39:30). The images are filled with meaning. Each animal is unique; each has its strength; each has its weakness. God cares for each of them, especially in their weakness. The ostrich, for example, is a proud and foolish bird who lacks a maternal instinct. Unlike other birds:

> . . . she leaves her eggs on the ground,
> And warms them in the dust;
> She forgets that a foot may crush them,
> Or that a wild beast may break them.
> She treats her young harshly,
> as though they were not hers . . . .
> (Job 39:14–16)

Yet, despite her lack of wisdom and understanding, God has endowed her with speed of foot that makes her the fastest bird on earth.

> When she lifts herself on high,
> She scorns the horse and its rider.
> (Job 39:18)

Job gets God's message. Before the mystery and the wonder of God's creative power, control, and care, he no longer doubts that God knows what He is doing. So, when God invites him to correct, rebuke, or answer Him, Job can only mumble:

> Behold, I am vile;
> What shall I answer You?
> I lay my hand over my mouth.
> Once I have spoken,
>   but I will not answer;
> Yes, twice,
>   but I will proceed no further.
> (Job 40:4–5)

Contrary to some interpretations of Job's submission, he is not beaten down like a whipped dog. Rather, he bows in reverential awe before the mystery and the majesty of Almighty God. No longer is he a self-righteous "know-it-all." With repentance, humility, and wisdom he says, "I shut my mouth."

God Speaks to Our Fears

In spite of Job's repentance and humility, another unspoken question lurks behind his complaint. Deep within his being is the fear, *"Does God really have control over all the circumstances of life?"* At one time or another, everyone who suffers asks the same question. We wonder if there is some small segment of the universe where God's power is limited. Otherwise, if He really cared, He would not let the innocent suffer. We simply cannot reconcile the suffering of the innocent with the goodness of God. Without an answer, we live with the fear that God lacks either the control or the care to handle all the circumstances which we face as human beings.

In response to Job's implied question, God again speaks out of the whirlwind:

> Now prepare yourself like a man;
> I will question you,
>   and you shall answer Me:
> (Job 40:7)

Although still using questions for His inquiry, God adds an ingenious teaching tactic to His speaking. Further complimenting Job's intelligence, He asks his servant to role-play His decision-making in the moral dilemmas with which God must deal. "What would you do if you were God?" is a question worthy of being asked each time we face the fear that our suffering might be out of His control or care. Specifically, God asks Job:

> Would you indeed annul My
>   judgment?
> Would you condemn Me
>   that you may be justified?
> Have you an arm like God?
> Or can you thunder with a voice like
>   His?
> Then adorn yourself
>   with majesty and splendor,
> And array yourself
>   with glory and beauty.
> (Job 40:8–10)

Three test questions follow. First, God asks Job, *"Would you crush the wicked if you were God?"* If you would:

> Then I will also confess to you
> That your own right hand can save
>   you.
> (Job 40:14)

Job is caught in his own trap of logic. If he were to play God and bring immediate judgment to the wicked, how would he escape? The truth comes home to him. Job has called for the justice of God to be exercised on his behalf with the hope of justification, but the fact is that he would be subject to God's wrath because he shares the sin of humanity.

A larger truth looms before us. Wherever and whenever

we human beings assume the role of God in passing judgment and meting out punishment against the wicked, we invite the wrath of God upon our heads as well. It is sad but true that the greatest atrocities in human history have been carried out in the name of God. Across the world at the present time, most of the wars being fought between and within nations are religious in nature. Hatred fueled by a righteous cause is the most vicious of all. If God allowed us to have our way with those whom we identify as the wicked of the earth, there would be no patience with those who do not measure up to our standard. And there would be no forgiveness for those who sinned! Job can draw his own conclusion: Except for God's patience with the wicked, there would be no hope of forgiveness for anyone, including himself!

God's second question for Job seems far-fetched at first. Showing Job a monstrous animal called a "behemoth" or hippopotamus, He implies the question, "*If you were God, would you create the ugly and the useless?*" In a picturesque description of the hippopotamus, its anatomy, its habitat, and its behavior, God recreates the image of a lovable, ugly monster who is content to eat, play, sleep, and swim without a care in the world.

> Indeed the river may rage,
> Yet he is not disturbed;
> He is confident, though the Jordan
>   gushes into his mouth,
> Though he takes it in his eyes,
> Or one pierces his nose with a snare.
> (Job 40:23–24)

In its own ludicrous way, the hippopotamus is a perfect example of trust in God even though it may be considered useless and ugly.

On a recent trip to Africa, I traipsed up and down the jungle path next to a waterhole trying to find the hippopotamus who lived there. I wanted to see for myself if God's description was accurate. Finally, a boisterous snort came from an island of reeds in the middle of the waterhole and a clumsy hippo belly-flopped into the water creating waves that upset the birds feeding on the pond and even the crocodile sunning on the shore. What a laughable, awkward monstrosity! Then and there I decided that God had a sense of humor because He created the hippopotamus. With Job, I expect that I would have canceled the creation of the hippopotamus for aesthetic and utilitarian reasons. But wait. God tells Job that the hippo is ". . . the first of the ways of God"—first of His creation, first of His care, and first of His love (Job 40:19). In other words, we need the hippo to show how God loves the seemingly ugly and the useless.

The lesson of the hippopotamus has contemporary application. As medical science saves more and more babies who are hopelessly deformed or retarded, there is the question of whether or not the same life-saving measures should be used for them as would be used for a healthy child whose life is at stake. How will we treat the ugly and the useless?

At the other end of the life spectrum is the reality that medical science is prolonging life so that persons who live to be 100 years old represent one of the fastest-growing age groups in the nation. Some think these aging people can no longer contribute to the goals of our utilitarian society. Should they be treated as choice persons of God's creation— or as candidates for merciful death? How will we treat the "ugly" and the "useless"?

Still another current example comes from our local scene. As developers are renovating the old downtown section of our community, they propose that "street people" be barred from the area because they are bad for business. A parallel proposal is that the Salvation Army move to the suburbs and take the "street people" with them. Without a doubt, these people are the dregs of society—ugly and useless in the eyes of man. But, in the eyes of God, are they the "hippos" of humanity—created by Him and loved by Him? If so, God's question is also asked of us, "Will you eliminate the ugly and the useless?" Job knows the answer and so do we. If we eliminate the ugly and the useless, whether in the animal world or among people, we do not know God's love. For Job especially, this lesson had meaning. Due to his suffering, he had taken his place among the ugly and the useless.

God's third question is the most penetrating of all. He shifts His image-making from the hippopotamus to the crocodile. The two animals are opposites. Whereas the hippopotamus looks lovable and innocent, even though ugly and useless, the crocodile is the personification of evil. No animal is more vicious, unpredictable, or incorrigible. In fact, when I asked a native of Florida to define the difference between an alligator and a crocodile, he told me that an alligator will attack a human being only if provoked while a crocodile will attack at any time. Perhaps this is why God goes to great lengths and minute details in His description of the crocodile as a creature about which nothing good can be said:

> On earth there is nothing like him,
> Which is made without fear.
> He beholds every high thing;
> He is king over all the children of
>   pride.
>
> (Job 41:33–34)

From the Satanic likeness of the crocodile comes God's third and final question to Job, *"If you were God, would you eliminate evil from the face of the earth?"* Undoubtedly, God could do it, but what would be lost? For one thing, we all have the root of evil in our nature, God would have to destroy His whole creation—including us. For another thing, our minds comprehend what is good because we also know what is evil. Most of all, if God wiped out evil from the earth, we would never understand the meaning of His grace—God's unmerited favor. To preserve our freedom, show His love, and offer His grace, God permits evil to exist, but never to conquer us. As powerful as the crocodile may be, God reminds Job: "Everything under heaven is Mine" (Job 41:11).

Job's nimble mind is quick to get the point. At the same time that he is humbled by God's greatness, he sees hope in His goodness. Job does not get the answer he wants, but he does get the answer he needs. By deep and searching questions, then, God leads Job to understand Who He is—The God of All Creation and The God of Every Contingency!

God is all-wise. If He had contested with Job over the question "Why?" their conversation would have been deadlocked. The pros and cons of a logical argument cannot account for the mystery of the universe or the paradox of truth. God, therefore, chooses to lead Job one question at a time to see the transcending vision of His wisdom and His love. Not that the question "Why?" is unimportant, but for people of faith, the question "Who?" is most important. Nietzsche said, "If we know 'Why?' we can bear any 'What?'" His philosophy spawned the Holocaust. For this reason, God leads Job toward the faith position, "If we know 'Who?' we can bear any 'What?'"

Current management theory has come full circle to make visionary leadership the key to empowering people and transforming organizations. For years, effective leadership was identified as process more than purpose. Traits of leaders were analyzed by computerized statistics and summarized in mathematical models. Something was missing. Finally, the students of organizations realized that an intuitive eye to the future coupled with a commitment to people and values represented the mysterious stuff out of which legendary leaders were made. Their vision for the future is more often a story than a statistic and more frequently a dream than a plan, but people are motivated to follow and energies are mobilized for action. The questions "Why? What? How?" and "When?" must still be asked by effective leaders, but the question "Who?" must precede them all.

Jesus could not have survived without the transcending vision of His Father. Even though He had the advantage of knowing why He suffered, Jesus' final test in the Garden of Gethsemane is the test of trust. Out of soul-rending trauma, He prayed, "Father, all things are possible for You. Take this cup away from Me; nevertheless, not what I will, but what You will" (Mark 14:36).

Hidden in these words are the same questions of doubt and fear that plagued Job and all who suffer. Does God really know what He is doing? Is God really in control of all life's circumstances? Or to put the question into God's vivid image of evil, "Will the crocodile win?" Because no one had tested the power of death and hell before, Jesus had no assurance that He would rise as conqueror except for His trust in God the Father. For Him, for Job, and for us, if we know "Who" God is, we can bear the suffering of "What?" and the mystery of "Why?"

At long last, Job is ready to answer God.

12

How Sufferers See

When we suffer and ask "Why?", it is time for seeing—more clearly and more completely than ever before. Pain has a way of sharpening the senses, focusing our attention, and enlarging our vision.

The perspective of pain amazes me. Just the other day I wrote down a memorable query voiced by a woman who is suffering from inoperable cancer. She has reached the stage where her bowels are blocked and vomiting is constant. During a call to her doctor she asked, "Can you become dehydrated by tears?" Despite her pain and exhaustion, she "sees" through her suffering with pathos and humor.

Job is another person who sees through suffering. He is quick to learn what God is saying to him. After drawing a picture of the crocodile as the personification of evil, God makes His point with Job:

> He beholds every high thing;
> He is king over all the children of
>   pride.
>
> (Job 41:34)

The word "pride" stings Job. For the first time, he fully realizes where he is wrong. Like a chess player throwing up his hands and exclaiming, "Checkmate," Job interrupts God to recite what he has learned in answer to God's question, "Who am I?" His answer is an affirmation of his new-found level of faith:

> I have heard You by the hearing
>   of the ear,
> But now my eye sees You.
>   (Job 42:5)

As with every human being who has ever seen God, Job also sees himself. He concludes his brief and final speech with a confession of his unworthiness and an act of contrition:

> Therefore I abhor myself,
> And repent in dust and ashes.
>   (Job 42:6)

On the pivot between Job's affirmation of faith and his confession of need is his insight into the way he knows God. Before he suffered, Job says he had heard about God "by the hearing of the ear." After God spoke to him, however, he says, "But now my eye sees You." Through suffering, Job's eyes are opened. He sees God wholly and himself clearly. He speaks now with the language of the eyes.

The Language of the Eyes

Ears and eyes have special meaning in Scripture. Hearing with the ears is *conceptual*. Ears are the symbol of rational understanding with a certain detachment from the subject under consideration. Only the mind is involved. Seeing with the eyes, however, is *perceptual*. The total being is involved— mind, emotions, and will. As Jesus said:

> The lamp of the body is the eye.
> If therefore your eye is good, your
> whole body will be full of light.
> But if your eye is bad, your whole
> body will be full of darkness. If therefore

> the light that is in you is darkness, how
> great is that darkness!
>
> (Matt. 6:22–23)

When I instruct someone how to take a picture with my
Polaroid camera, I say, "What you see is what you get." Jesus
is giving similar instructions to us about the spiritual focus of
the eye: "What you see is what you are."

Our eyes reveal our souls. *Through* them is the entry of
light or darkness; *from* them is the reflection of light or darkness; *in* them is the image of light or darkness. Much has been
written about the language of the body. The way in which a
person responds physically in gestures, posture, blushes, and
twitches is a nonverbal language of its own—so much so that
our "body language" can speak more loudly than our words.

Our eyes are even more eloquent. Poets have always
recognized the "language of the eyes." Shakespeare wrote:

> The heart's still rhetoric disclosed with eyes.
> (*Love's Labour's Lost.* Act ii, sc. 1, 1. 229).

> Methought all his senses were lock'd in his eye,
> As jewels in crystal for some prince to buy.
> (*Love's Labour's Lost.* Act ii, sc. 1, 1. 242).

> Sometimes from her eyes
> I did receive fair speechless messages.
> (*The Merchant of Venice.* Act i, sc.1, 1. 163).

> She speaks, yet she says nothing: what of
> that?
> Her eye discourses; I will answer it.
> (*Romeo and Juliet.* Act ii, sc. 2, 1. 12).

> There's language in her eye.
> (*Troilus and Cressida.* Act iv, sc. 5, 1. 55).

Far less classic, but no less meaningful is the popular
song of the 1940s which tells how the language of the eyes
can override the language of the lips:

> Your lips tell me "No, No,"
> But there's "Yes, Yes" in your eyes.

Learning to read the language of the eyes is an art in
itself. For a long time, I wondered why Arab businessmen

always seem to wear sunglasses, whether indoors or out-of-doors, summer or winter, daytime or nighttime. I assumed that they had become accustomed to protecting themselves against the brilliance of the Middle Eastern sun. Then I learned the real reason. Unlike Western businesspeople who do their bargaining across huge tables, the Arabs sit face to face and do their business eyeball-to-eyeball within inches of each other! Thus, they become experts in reading the eyes of their competitors, constantly on the alert for telltale signs of lying, fear, anger, compromise, defeat, and determination. Sunglasses are worn to keep their eyes from betraying their lips.

Long ago, I stumbled upon the secret of reading people through the language of their eyes. For my annual physical checkup, I went to a doctor whom I have known as a classmate and friend. All during the time that he poked and probed at me, he kept up an incessant, excited chatter about his successes in the stock market. At first he confused me because I went to him for medical, not financial, advice. Furthermore, I knew that he had come from a family that was as poor as proverbial church mice.

He had struggled in poverty through college and medical school. Now, he stood over me in a white coat, a prominent physician in the community, chattering about the stock market. As I looked up, our eyes met. I shall never forget what I saw. Through the gleam in his eye, I saw clear through to his soul. Under the white coat and behind the professional confidence, a poor boy still dreamed of being rich!

Ever since then, when we meet, I ask him, "Doctor, how are you doing in the market?" Like snapping on a light switch, the gleam in his eyes flashes and the chatter begins.

Since that time, I have worked to perfect my "gleam-in-the-eye" technique. When I interview job candidates, I ask question after question until I see the gleam. Just yesterday, a faculty prospect sat in my office. We talked about a variety of professional matters standard for such an interview. Then, I asked him point blank, "Where's the gleam in your eye?" The light came on as he answered, "Our new baby is first. He's a miracle because the doctor told us we could never have children. Then, I want to write. Our spoken words are temporary, but our writing is permanent. I dream of being an evangelical Christian who influences biblical scholarship through my writing."

We spent the rest of the time talking about the personal priority of our families and the professional priority of our writing. When we meet again, I will ask first, "How's your son?" and then, "How's your writing?" If he joins our faculty, he has my assurance that I will help him follow the gleam in his eye.

The language of the eyes leads us to ask, "What does Job mean when he answers God, 'But now my eye sees you'?" Instead of the look of pride do we detect now a gleam in Job's eye that is a reflection of his soul—seeing God wholly and himself clearly?

Seeing God Wholly

How do we know God? Job illustrates that we can know Him through the exercise of reason, or, as he puts it, the "hearing of the ear." By its very nature, reason keeps God at a distance as a detached object to be studied but not experienced. Reason also restricts our knowledge of God to a partial view of His Person. There is little room for the range of God's emotions or the freedom of His will. But our greatest fault in knowing God by the "hearing of the ear" is to assume that He is like us—a Person subject to the rules of reason which we conceive, and accountable to the logical deductions that we make. Such an assumption leads to the sin of pride— the very trap into which Job fell.

Many theologians are still guilty of the sin of pride. A generation does not pass except some theologian tries to define God and Jesus Christ in rational, human terms. A century ago biblical scholars became enamored with the budding field of psychiatry and, following the theory of that discipline, concluded that Jesus was a psychotic with messianic fantasies and self-destructive tendencies. In our generation, we have survived the historical Jesus, the demythologized Jesus, the Death of God, and the Myth of God Incarnate. But neither God nor Jesus can be explained or extinguished by the flitting conclusions of human reason. That would be like fireflies trying to put out the sun.

We should have learned our lesson from Job. Reason took him a long way toward understanding God, but it failed when Job assumed that he could argue with God on equal terms and according to his own ground rules. As we have already learned, God allows us to ask the question "Why?" when we suffer, but if we demand an answer on our terms, we are like Job—guilty of the sin of pride.

When our suffering is total, partial answers will not do. We must see God wholly. Through the totality of suffering, Job realizes that he has never seen through to God in His wholeness. When he confesses to God, "But now my eye sees You," Job is testifying to an experience of viewing God as a Person with whom he can relate rather than an object to be studied or a mind with which to compete.

In a lecture entitled "Seeing Through the Eye" Malcolm Muggeridge gives us some insight into the meaning of Job's words. From the poem by Edmund Blake, Muggeridge quotes:

> This Life's dim windows of the soul
> Distorts the Heavens from Pole to Pole,
> And leads you to believe a lie,
> When you see with, not through, the eye.[1]

Television is the special target of Muggeridge's criticism. He contends that the tube induces us to "see with the eyes" to secular fantasy and dissuades us from "seeing through the eyes" to spiritual reality. Quite in contrast to the pride of rational thought which leads us to believe that we are like God, Muggeridge damns television for exploiting our senses and leading us to the sin of lust which makes us animals.

Muggeridge gives us insight into Job's confession which draws the distinction between knowing about God through some isolated part of our human nature and seeing Him as a whole Person in His divine nature. "Seeing through the eye" to God, according to Muggeridge, ". . . is to grasp the significance of what is seen, to see it in relation to the totality of God's creation . . . ."[2]

This definition is consistent with Job's confession. We can accurately translate his words:

> But now I see *through* to you with my eyes.

No longer is Job asking the question, *"Why do I suffer?"* It is still important for learning, but it is not essential for faith. Job is now captivated by God's answer to His own question, "WHO AM I?" No longer does Job want to prance like a prince into the presence of God or demand that God come down and answer him like an attorney in a courtroom. Having seen his suffering in relationship to the Person of God, Job affirms his new-found level of faith by answering God's question "WHO AM I?"

> I know that You can do everything,
> And that no purpose of Yours can be
>   withheld from You.
> You asked, "Who is this who hides
>   counsel without knowledge?"
> Therefore I have uttered
>   what I did not understand,
> Things too wonderful for me,
>   which I did not know.
> Listen, please, and let me speak;
> You said, "I will question you,
>   and you shall answer Me."
>   (Job 42:2–4)

Within these words is the affirmation of faith that will sustain us during the times when we ask "Why?"—whatever the cause, nature, or timing of our suffering. It cannot be recited glibly; in fact, it can be spoken only out of the experience of asking, "Why do I suffer?" and seeing through to the Person of God. We must come to the place of saying:

I KNOW THAT YOUR *POWER* CAN DO ANYTHING FOR ME.
I KNOW THAT YOUR *PURPOSE* WILL BE FULFILLED FOR ME.
I KNOW THAT YOUR *WAYS* ARE TOO WONDERFUL FOR ME.

Long before I studied Job, I learned the value of this affirmation of faith for people who are suffering. As a hospital chaplain, I frequently ministered to patients who entertained fantasies about their healing, others who were filled with bitterness against God, and still others who gave up without a fight. The result was the same. Their attitudes worked against their healing. If, however, through the ministry of listening, counseling, prayer, and Scripture, we could lead them to see through the eyes of faith to the greatness and goodness of God, their spiritual healing led the way for their physical and emotional healing. Not once do I remember a patient being healed by drawing a conclusion about the answer, *"Why do I suffer?"*, but I can cite case after case of persons—some who were healed, others who continued to suffer, and still others who died—with the gleam in their eyes of "seeing through" to God.

The key to understanding the gleam in Job's eye is his *sense of wonder.* Fear dictated his faith when he knew God only through the hearing of the ears. But now when he sees through to God, wonder is the language of his eyes.

Malcolm Muggeridge attributes his spiritual conversion to the wonder that he saw in the eyes of Christians. As a crusty and cantankerous journalist, he put Christianity into the category of another philosophy of life which he had tested and rejected. Neither the words nor the writing of Christian witness fazed him. Then, on an assignment with the British Broadcasting Company, Muggeridge traveled to Jerusalem to film a television documentary on the Holy Land. While he was on location, a group of Christians on pilgrimage appeared. Muggeridge had heard their prayers and hymns before, but he had never seen the gleam of wonder in their eyes. Afterward he wrote:

> . . . seeing a party of Christian pilgrims at one of their Shrines, their faces bright with faith, their voices as they sang, so evidently and joyously aware of their Savior's nearness, I understood that for them the Shrine was authentic. Their faith made it so. Similarly, I too became aware that there really had been a man, Jesus, who was God: I was conscious of His presence.[3]

More often than not the gleam of wonder in our eyes is the language of our souls.

Seeing Ourselves Clearly

When we see God wholly, we also see ourselves clearly. Job joins with patriarchs, priests, prophets, and apostles who saw themselves reflected in their own vision of God. With one voice, they cry out:

> Therefore I abhor myself,
> And repent in dust and ashes.
> (Job 42:6)

How sad it is that some critics of Job make this a debasing experience for the man and a justifying act for God. Nothing is farther from the truth. Even though Job needs to bow and repent of his pride, he is not a maggot groveling in the dust or a wimp quivering in the ashes. By his own free choice, he confesses his sinfulness and repents of his pride. Reaching down into the dust and ashes of his altar of suffering, he pours them over his head as the symbol of his penitence.

Yet, in the language of his eyes, there is a gleam. To his earlier affirmation of faith, Job can now add:

I KNOW THAT YOUR *WILL* IS GOOD FOR ME.
I KNOW THAT YOUR *LOVE* IS HOPE FOR ME.

So Job bows in humility to identify with all of humankind and repents with hope for all who suffer.

A Personal Note to All Who Suffer

Earlier, I confessed an open wound left over from my expectation that I would be named as Secretary of Education in the first cabinet of the Reagan Administration. Bit by bit God has healed this wound by helping me see through to His Person and purpose. For three days after the ego-shaking news of my rejection, I jogged along the shores of Puget Sound shouting my anger into the winds and demanding that God answer my question "Why?" On the fourth day, God spoke clearly, ". . . I know the thoughts that I think toward you, . . . thoughts of peace and not of evil, to give you a future and a hope" (Jer. 29:11).

Peace settled over my spirit for the first time in days. Intellectually, at least, I accepted the fact that God knew what He was doing.

The promise held until I went back to Washington for the first time after the decision. Sitting in my hotel room, I saw a local telecast which opened the wound once again. When the camera scanned the Cabinet Room in the White House, it focused on each of the brass nameplates on the back of the cabinet officers' chairs. Like Baby Bear in *Goldilocks and the Three Bears,* I pouted, "Someone's sitting in my chair." Shortly thereafter I revealed my bleeding and festering wound to Senator Mark Hatfield, who had nominated me in the first place. The Senator became my Elihu.

After listening graciously and intently, he told me his own story. Although the details must be reserved for his memoirs, the Senator recalled the time when he and his wife waited through the night for the expected call to be the running mate for Richard Nixon. The call never came. At the last second the fickle winds of political maneuvering changed direction in favor of Spiro Agnew. Think of it. If Mark Hatfield had been nominated that night either Watergate would not have happened—or he would have become President of the United States!

Why? Does God know what He is doing? While Senator Hatfield had no answers, he had peace, a peace that passed his understanding. With him, the course of the nation was at stake. With me, it was just a brass plate on the back of a walnut chair. I left his office shamed by the smallness of my sight, but seeing clearly for the first time. *God knows what He is doing.*

Many times since that experience, I have recited Job's affirmation of new faith. For all who go through suffering, ask "Why?", and then get a glimpse of Who God is, it is our promise of a future filled with hope:

> *I know that Your power can do anything for me.*
> *I know that Your purpose will be fulfilled for me.*
> *I know that Your ways are too wonderful for me.*
> *I know that Your will is good for me.*
> *I know that Your love is hope for me.*

With this confession, we bow with Job in the dust and ashes not like a worm, but like a phoenix bird—ready to rise to new splendor of spirit—by the grace of God.

"So Job died, old
and full of days."
—Author of Job

13
How Grace Transforms

When we suffer and ask "Why?", the only answer to our question is God's transforming grace. Job experienced this truth the hard way. In a long and torturous journey through physical pain, emotional despair, and spiritual loneliness, he dead-ended into his own self-righteousness. As a show of his pride, Job even dared to say that he could enter the presence of God like a prince coming before the king. With equal audacity he demanded that God come down to his level and defend Himself on Job's turf and terms. Somewhere on the way through this struggle, the question "Why?" was lost in a contest of wills.

Job had the arrogance to infer that he was right and God was wrong. Deeper down, he also entertained the notion that he was as wise and good as God Himself. It is no wonder God spoke to him out of a whirlwind. A still, small voice would not do. Job's rationalistic faith had led him into a power struggle with God—not unlike the conflict that each of us knows when we pit our wills against God's will. So, we are not surprised that when God speaks He ignores Job's original question, "Why do I suffer?" and instead, overwhelms Job with probe after probe into the question, "WHO AM I?"

After the first round of these questions, Job answers with reverential awe, "I shut my mouth." After the second round, Job joins the ranks of those who have seen through to God. He not only answers the question *"Who is God?"* with an affirmation of new-found faith but also turns the coin to ask the same question about himself: *"Who am I?"* Then seeing God wholly and himself clearly, Job bows before the greatness of God and repents of the pride that led him to believe he was as right, wise, and good as God. His ashheap becomes an altar as Job pours over his head the dust of his humanity and the charred remains of his pride.

Without the grace of God, Job must remain in the dust and ashes abhorring himself and repenting of his sins. Perhaps this is why so many critical scholars of the Book of Job insist that the Epilogue of Restoration (Job 42:7–17) be cut out of the text. Either they do not understand the meaning of grace or they fail to see the redemptive thread that runs through the Book of Job and leads to Jesus Christ. Their argument is that the restoration of Job reads like a fairytale that ends unrealistically with the line, "And so they lived happily ever after."

As another reason for excising the Epilogue, critics argue that Job's restoration after his repentance only proves that Eliphaz, Bildad, and Zophar were right all along. After all, doesn't Job's repentance and return to prosperity prove that God's justice works on the formula that sin results in suffering and righteousness brings blessing? More than that, doesn't Job's restoration to prosperity after repentance prove that Satan is justified in asking the question which provoked Job's suffering in the first place, "Does Job serve God for nought?"

If you follow this argument, God must have felt guilty about taking Satan's bait and so, when Job repents of being driven to the sin of self-righteousness, He responds by doubling his prosperity, his family, and his years. In this case, it is God, not Job, who needs to be forgiven!

As a child Elie Wiesel survived the Nazi Holocaust. For ten years he could not speak or write of the experience because of his pain and anguish. When he did write, Wiesel entitled his first book *Night*. He tells of seeing a child twist and turn on the gallows for three days before dying. Forced to watch the innocent victim suffer and die, Wiesel hears a voice within him asking, "Where's God? Where's God?" The answer comes back, "God is on the gallows." For Wiesel, God dies with the innocent who suffer. Or at best, God must join Job, repenting in the dust and ashes.

As the alternative to leaving God and Job in the dust and ashes, some playwrights and authors have rewritten the ending of the story. Archibald MacLeish retells the story of Job in his stageplay *J. B.* The final scene shows J. B. and his wife reflecting upon the experience of his suffering. She says to him, "You wanted justice, didn't you? There isn't any . . . there is only love."

God and Satan, watching the scene from high above the stage, are both baffled. Together they ask:

> Who plays the hero, God or him?
> Is God to be forgiven?
> Isn't He? Job is innocent,
> You may remember.

J. B. forgives God and as the curtain falls his wife wonders aloud:

> The candles in the churches are out,
> The stars have gone out in the sky,
> Blow on the coals of the heart
> And we'll see by and by.[1]

The message? With God needing forgiveness, human love is the only prospect for hope.

Rabbi Harold Kushner, author of the bestseller *When Bad Things Happen to Good People*, has also rewritten the ending of the Book of Job. After his infant son Aaron was stricken with the dread disease of progeria or premature aging, Rabbi Kushner suffered with the child until he died an old, gray, and wrinkled man two days after his fourteenth birthday. Throughout those years Rabbi Kushner kept pushing his faith for an answer to the question, "Why do the innocent suffer?" Because no answer came, Kushner

concluded that God is limited in His power to deal with the
suffering of the innocent. Therefore, he shifts the burden of
love to those who suffer. Of them, he asks:

> Are you capable of forgiving and accepting in love a world which
> has disappointed you by not being perfect . . . ?
> Are you capable of forgiving and loving the people around you,
> even if they hurt you and let you down by not being perfect . . . ?
> Are you capable of forgiving and loving God even when you have
> found out that He is not perfect . . . ?
> And if you can do these things, will you be able to recognize that
> the ability to forgive and the ability to love are the weapons God has
> given to us to live fully, bravely, and meaningfully in this less-than-
> perfect world?[2]

Kushner's answer to the question, "Why do the innocent
suffer?" is to conclude that God and the world that He created are both imperfect. He must be forgiven and the suffering of His world must be tolerated. Forgiveness and love are
our only hope. So, reaching for these resources within himself, Kushner's final word is, "I think of Aaron and all that
his life taught me and I realize how much I have lost and how
much I have gained. Yesterday seems less painful and I am
not afraid of tomorrow."[3]

Out of the dust and ashes of his suffering, Kushner's
only hope is to muster the courage to go on living.

Grace is missing from all the rewritten endings of the
Book of Job. If, however, you read the story of Job's suffering as a journey toward God's transforming grace, the whole
scene changes. The drama is not complete without the ending as it is written. It loses its prophetic promise of the coming of Jesus Christ and the redemptive thread that confirms
the Book of Job as part and parcel of the inspired Word of
God. Moreover, unless we read the restoration of Job as
evidence of God's transforming grace, we leave Him in the
dust and ashes with Job—limited in power, imperfect in
character, and in need of our forgiveness. If this is true,
what word of hope do we have for those who suffer and ask
"Why?"

> Give up on God?
> Forgive Him for being imperfect?
> Blow on the coals of our heart?

Wait for the sweet by-and-by?

Face tomorrow without fear?

None of these answers is sufficient. None of them is true. Unless the ending of the Book of Job is read as a story of grace, we leave God and all who suffer in the dust and ashes without hope.

Only with grace do we have a word of hope for all who suffer. When God spoke to Job about the hippopotamus and the crocodile, He revealed His love and forgiveness as expressions of His grace. When Job bowed before God and repented of his pride, he put himself at the mercy of the Father. Forfeiting all claim to wisdom or righteousness, Job has no merit of his own. In dust and ashes, he confesses that he deserves the wrath of God. Except for grace, he has no hope. But by grace he has the promise of redemption and restoration. For all who suffer, then, the final question is not *"Why?"* but *"Who?"*

Grace for Grace

Grace is free, but never easy or cheap. Contrary to those who assume that God restores Job by a wave of a magical wand, Scripture tells us that Job is still on the ashheap waiting for God to make His move. Job is not restored magically or immediately. Instead, he has to wait while God goes back to Eliphaz, Bildad, and Zophar with a word for them. Speaking to their spokesman, Eliphaz, God says,

> My wrath is aroused against you and your two friends, for you have not spoken of Me what is right, as My servant Job has.
> Now therefore, take for yourselves seven bulls and seven rams, go to My servant Job, and offer up for yourselves a burnt offering; and My servant Job shall pray for you. For I will accept him, lest I deal with you according to your folly; because you have not spoken of Me what is right, as My servant Job has.
>
> (Job 42:7–8)

Startling words! God accepts Job who attacked Him and rejects the three who defended Him. Will we ever learn the lesson? God does not want to be defended by us. He would rather hear us angrily crying *"Why?"* than assuming that we have all the answers. Job questioned God, but he never played God. So, despite shutting his mouth and opening his eyes, God still calls Job "My servant" three times in His commands to Eliphaz. What an example of His grace! Although Job almost gave up on God, God never gave up on him. Despite Job's anger, doubt, belligerence, and pride, God still claims, loves, and praises him. As costly as it is, only grace can do that.

Cheap grace is the bane of our contemporary spiritual existence. In contrast with those who would leave Job on the ashheap in a posture of submission and repentance, too often we skip the ashheap altogether. Much popular preaching shortcircuits the redemptive process by skipping from God's revelation to our restoration. We want prosperity without repentance. It is a manmade contingency that makes the sense of sin dull and the cost of grace cheap. We forget the "Lamb that was slain from the foundation of the world." Even though Job lived centuries before the coming of Christ, the grace of God given to him when he deserved nothing is the same costly grace that bought our salvation in the death of Jesus Christ.

How do we know that the gift of grace transformed Job's life? We read that God "accepted Job"—this is grace in itself because Job's behavior warranted the wrath of justice. But there is even greater evidence of transforming grace in Job's life. He gave grace as well as received it. This is the real story of his restoration—not just the evidence of grace received in the doubling of his fortune, fame, and family, but the proof of grace that he showed to others. As always, we know that we are restored by grace when our relationships with foes, friends, and family are transformed by grace.

Grace Seeks No Revenge

After God tells Eliphaz that His wrath is aroused against him and his friends because they misrepresented Him, He offers them grace if they will make a sacrifice for their sin and ask Job to pray for them. What an ego-shattering command! All their pious and prejudicial judgments against Job must be swallowed in the dust and ashes of their own repentance. The test of grace, however, rests with Job. Will he pray for his friends who betrayed him?

Put yourself in the same spot. Justice says that these turncoat friends do not deserve Job's prayers. Rather than comforting Job, they attacked him and accused him of every sin they could imagine to protect the orthodoxy of power. Who would blame Job if he turned his back and refused to pray for them? Or at least made them suffer a bit by letting them cower at his feet and beg for forgiveness before he prays for them?

The God of grace has made Job a man of grace. Instead of seeking revenge against his friends who betrayed him, he prays for their forgiveness and they are accepted by God. It may sound easy, but I am sure that Job had second thoughts before he prayed. Retaliation is always a temptation for a person who has power over the destiny of others.

As a college president, there have been times when I have been wounded by friends whom I thought were loyal. When the time comes for their promotion or praise, the temptation is to get even. On one occasion, I remember suffering under unfair criticism for an administrative decision I had made. Persons whom I thought were friends had turned my administrative decision into a personalized issue. I had the choice of retaliation by direct counterattack or indirect discrimination against them in promotion policies.

About that time, Ray Stedman came to campus for a Spiritual Emphasis Week. In his first address, he spoke on the text, "Vengeance is mine, I will repay, says the Lord." His exposition emphasized the fact that whenever we seek vengeance for wrong, we commit the sin of overkill and, in the long run, damage ourselves as well as the person against whom we seek revenge. He went on to appeal for us to show the grace to others that God has shown to us. I took that message seriously and refused to seek revenge upon those whom I felt had wronged me, even though I had in my hands the power to do so. The lesson has stood me well. A working principle of my administration is that I will never use my executive power to retaliate against someone whom I feel has wronged me. Time and time again I have prayed for grace in such moments, but to my knowledge, I have never violated the principle.

One of the books with which I am most proud to have my name associated is the reprint of *The DeShazer Story.* Jake DeShazer gained fame as a member of Jimmy Doolittle's crew that made a daring bombing raid against Tokyo during World War II. After thirty seconds over Tokyo, Jake's plane was shot down and he spent almost thirty months in a Japanese prison camp, tortured within a breath of death.

During those months of suffering, DeShazer received a Bible. He read it, believed it, and became a vital Christian whose faith sustained him when death seemed imminent.

With the end of the war liberation came and DeShazer enrolled at Seattle Pacific University with one goal in mind. He intended to go back to his captors and preach the gospel of Jesus Christ. While patiently working his way through college as a married veteran, Jake rekindled the missionary spirit which had motivated the founding of Seattle Pacific University.

After graduation, he went back to Japan as a fledgling missionary. Hundreds and thousands of Japanese flocked to hear him. Yet, Jake DeShazer is the most unlikely hero or evangelist. He is shy and self-effacing. His speech is halting and his thoughts are as simple as a child's.

The Japanese came only to hear the strange message of love from a man whom they had tortured. Once Jake began to speak, however, the Spirit took over. Two of the guards who had brutalized him heard his message along with scores of others who came forward to seek Jesus Christ as their Savior. Later, in a Tokyo stadium before thousands of people, Jake DeShazer, the Doolittle bomber, stood arm in arm with Commander Fuchida, leader of the Pearl Harbor attack, as brothers in Christ. Only God's grace can do that!

Note the sequence of Job's restoration. *"And the Lord restored* Job's losses *when he prayed for his friends.* Indeed, the Lord gave Job twice as much as he had before"* (Job 42:10, emphasis mine).

In one simple sentence, Satan's claim is refuted. Job did not serve God because of the blessings he received. Certainly, he struck no bargain with God guaranteeing him prosperity if he interceded for his friends. God's grace is given, not only independent of the merit of the receiver, but also without the guarantee of any return.

Grace Holds No Grudges

Fame follows fortune. The word that Job had returned to wealth with a doubled fortune must have been the talk of the country. In our day, he would have been featured on the cover of *Time* magazine as the Man of the Year. Such fame has its own magnetic pull. Needless to say, Job's family and friends, who had abandoned him when his fortunes were down, now return in droves to curry his favor.

> Then all his brothers, all his sisters, and all those who had been his acquaintances before, came to him and ate food with him in his house; and they consoled him and comforted him for all the adversity that the Lord had brought upon him. Each one gave him a piece of silver and each a ring of gold.
>
> (Job 42:11)

How sickening. Fair-weather family and friends come and go as fame rises and falls. Many politicians are victimized by their fame. When they are in power, everyone wants to be identified with them. Washington, D. C., for instance, is known for a disease called "Potomac Fever." It is an addiction to political power which turns on name-dropping and personal contacts. But political power is as fickle as fame. A politician out of power is a nonentity whom the press ignores and old friends bypass. This fact of life is so disgusting that many qualified people avoid politics in order to retain their independence and integrity. Sad as it may be, family and friends who abandon us in our suffering will return to comfort us when we are healed.

God is also a victim of fair-weather friends. Someone once said, "If I were God and had been treated the way we humans treat Him, I'd have kicked this old world to pieces a long time ago." Job had a right to feel the same way. Here were his hypocritical family and friends, returning to comfort and console him when he no longer needed it! As they moaned and groaned over his past distress, he might have

stopped them in their tracks by asking, "Where were you
when I needed you?" Certainly, Job remembered his plaintive cry for their help during his most desperate hour of
need:

> . . . I stand up in the congregation
> and cry out for help.
> I am a brother of jackals,
> And a companion of ostriches.
>   (Job 30:28–29)

This memory of his loneliness and humiliation had to
haunt him. Instead of receiving help from his brothers and
companions in the time of suffering, he had been abandoned
as a laughable, ludicrous creature not unlike the jackal and
the ostrich. Imagine how difficult it must have been for Job
to sit at dinner after his fortune and fame had been restored
with those same brothers and companions who had not only
abandoned him, but mocked him as well. Worse yet, Job had
to accept a piece of silver and a ring of gold from each of
them—gifts that he neither needed nor wanted.

What would you do? Justice says, "I have no food for
you." Justice says, "I don't need your comfort now." Justice
says, "Take your gifts and go."

Some years ago, I was among the hosts for Margaret
Mead, the renowned anthropologist, whom we honored with
a $25,000 award as a leader in the field of science. After her
lecture and the presentation of the award, the hosting committee had lunch high in the revolving restaurant of the
Space Needle in Seattle, Washington. As a personal gift to
her, we gave her a sterling silver replica of the Space Needle
giftwrapped in a silver foil package. Before Dr. Mead
opened her gift she laughed and said, "Do you know that the
final test given to British diplomats in training is to say
'Thank you' for a gift that they neither need nor want?"

Although she was delighted with her silver Space
Needle, I have never forgotten her question, "How do
you say 'Thank you' for a gift that you neither need nor
want?" That is more than a test of diplomacy; it is a test of
grace. "How do you say thank you to family and friends

who have abandoned you in suffering, but come back to insult your intelligence by eating your food, bemoaning your misfortune, and bringing you gifts *after* you are restored to health, wealth, and fame?"

Job gives us the answer. *Grace holds no grudges.* Because God accepted him despite his folly, Job accepts his family and friends despite their fickleness. Only grace can do that!

Grace Plays No Favorites

The economy of grace is multiple. God gives and gives and gives again. Of Job's later life we read, "Now the Lord blessed the latter days of Job more than his beginning . . ." (Job 42:12).

His wealth, his cattle, and his years are doubled. Even the number of his sons is doubled according to the most accurate translation of the text. Only the number of his daughters remains the same. He had three who died in the windstorm and three who are born in his later years. To our surprise, they are singled out by name and noted for the fact that they are the most beautiful women in the land. The first daughter is Jemimah, a name which means "turtledove," the most beautiful of songbirds. The next daughter is Keziah, which means "cinnamon," the most fragrant of all the spices of the East. Last comes Keren-Happuch, whose name means "horn of paint," the cosmetic case for beautifying the face among the women of the East. So, the names of Job's three daughters match their reputation as the most beautiful women of the land—beautiful in song, beautiful in smell, and beautiful in sight.

To each of these three daughters, Job gives an inheritance equal to their brothers (Job 42:15). Hidden within these words is one of the most significant and far-reaching truths in the Book of Job. We must remember that Job lived in a patriarchal age in which women were of no account. Job's wife, for instance, is not mentioned as a part of her husband's restoration. Yet, the fact that he had fourteen more sons and three more daughters tells us that she was waiting for Job to come home; and if we can believe the old adage, "Like mother, like daughter," she must have been a beautiful woman. Nevertheless, in the patriarchal culture of the East, daughters did not share in the family inheritance. Even later, when the Law of Moses was written, we read, "If a man dies and has no sons, then, you shall cause his inheritance to pass to his daughter" (Num. 27:8). So daughters had to wait in line for a share of the family inheritance and, even then, they received nothing unless there were no sons.

Job goes against the customs and the mores of his culture when he gives his three daughters full and equal shares of his inheritance while all his sons are still alive. According to tradition and law, they do not deserve it. Justice always says to the disinherited, "Wait in line." But grace answers, "Whosoever will."

By sharing his inheritance with his daughters, Job gives us another prophetic insight into God's redemptive plan. Grace makes no difference between men and women. Furthermore, in the symbol of the fourteen sons is foreseen the promise to Abraham that his seed shall be multiplied as the stars of the sky and the sand of the sea. But the daughters symbolize the Gentiles who do not share the promise given to Abraham and are outside his spiritual inheritance. According to the Law, daughters and Gentiles are like the dogs that get the crumbs from the table after the family has eaten.

Why then does Job break with tradition and the law? Grace has to be the answer. As God blessed Job with doubled wealth that he did not expect or deserve, Job in turn wants to share his wealth with all whom he loves. *Grace plays no favorites.* It is always breaking away from tradition and law as a gift to the least, the last, and the lost among us.

In a patriarchal age, grace gives to women;
In an adult culture, grace gives to children;
In an affluent society, grace gives to the poor;
In a "macho" world, grace gives to the weak;
In a Jewish nation, grace gives to Gentiles;
In a Christian community, grace gives to sinners.

Job's gift of grace to his daughters points to Christ's gift of salvation for all who believe. Especially those of us who feel spiritually disenfranchised by our background or spiritually disinherited by our nature, the message of the Book of Job is that God's grace is for us. If we are enemies of God, grace seeks no vengeance. If we are betrayers of God, grace holds no grudges. If we deserve nothing from God, grace plays no favorites.

Job's story, then, is our story—sooner or later, the story of every person on earth. When we suffer and ask "Why?" we embark upon a long and sometimes torturous journey of faith which can lead us to see through to God and receive the gift of His transforming grace. In turn, we become instruments of His grace—forgiving our enemies who attack us, accepting our family and friends who abandon us, and sharing our inheritance with those who deserve nothing. Out of our suffering comes the promise of John's witness to the coming Christ, "And of His fulness we have all received, and grace for grace" (John 1:16). Like the waves of the sea, grace is the inexhaustible gift that is given again and again for all who suffer.

> He giveth more grace when the burden grows greater,
> He sendeth more strength when the labors increase,
> To added affliction, He addeth His mercy,
> To multiplied trials, His multiplied peace.
>
> His love has no limit; His grace has no measure,
> His power has no boundary known unto men,
> For out of His infinite riches in Jesus,
> He giveth, and giveth, and giveth again.[4]

So ends the journey of Job. It began with the question "Why?"; it ends with the answer "Who?" It began with a discipline of hearing; it ends with the relationship of seeing. It began with a look of fear; it ends with a sense of wonder. It began with the ring of righteousness; it ends on the note of faith. It began with the thunder of God's power; it ends with the whisper of His grace.

All who suffer and ask "Why?" will take the same journey. Along the way there will be blind turns and hazardous intersections, despairing pits and dizzying heights, lonely stretches and lighted signposts. Eventually we will bow with Job on his ashheap, not unlike Pilgrim of Bunyan's tale bowing at the foot of the cross. When we do, there will be no thunder of God's power; we will hear only the whisper of His grace.

> O let me hear Your whisper,
> The Whisper of Your Grace.
> Hearing, I will see You
> and seeing,
> I am transformed!
> *—David L. McKenna*

Notes

Chapter 3

1. T. H. Holmes and M. Masuda, B. S. Dohrenwend and B. P. Dohrenwend, Eds. "Life Changes and Illness Susceptibility." Ch. in *Stressful Life Events: Their Nature and Effects* (New York: Wiley, 1974).

Chapter 4

1. Anton T. Boisen, *The Exploration of the Inner World* (New York: Harper Brothers Publishers, 1936) 1.
2. Soren Kierkegaard *The Sickness Unto Death* (Princeton: Princeton University Press, 1980) 37.

Chapter 5

1. William E. Hulme, *Dialogue of Despair* (Nashville: Abingdon Press, 1968) 19ff.

Chapter 6

1. C. S. Lewis, *A Grief Observed* (Winchester, Mass.: Faber & Faber) 5, 89.

Chapter 7

1. James W. Fowler, *The Stages of Faith Development* (New York: Harper and Row, 1976) 14–15.
2. Elliott Wright, *The Holy Company: Christian Heroes and Heroines* (New York: Macmillan Publishing Company, Inc., 1980), 1.

3. Hubert Mitchell and Annie Johnson Flint, "He Giveth More Grace" © 1941, renewed 1969 by Lillenas Publishing Company. Used by Permission. *Hymns and Faith and Life* (Winona Lake, Ind.: Light and Life Press and the Wesley Press, 1976).

Chapter 8

1. Andrew Watterson Blackwood, *The Protestant Pulpit* (New York: Abingdon-Cokesbury Press, 1947), 204.

Chapter 9

1. William Bridges, *Transitions: Making Sense of Life's Changes* (Reading, Mass.: Addison-Wesley, 1980).

Chapter 10

1. Paul Tournier, *Creative Suffering* (New York: Harper and Row, 1981), 81–82.
2. Loc. cit., 82–83.

Chapter 11

1. Meyer Friedman and Ray Rosenman, *Type "A" Behavior and Your Heart* (New York: Fawcett Crest Books, 1974), 84.

Chapter 12

1. Malcolm Muggeridge, *Christ and the Media* (Grand Rapids: William B. Eerdman's Publishing Company, 1977) 62–63.
2. Ibid.
3. Malcolm Muggeridge, *Jesus Rediscovered* (Garden City, N.Y.: Doubleday and Company, 1969), x.

Chapter 13

1. Archibald MacLeish, *J.B.* (Boston: Houghton Mifflin Co., 1956) 140ff.
2. Harold S. Kushner, *When Bad Things Happen to Good People* (New York: Avon Books, 1981) 147–48.
3. Ibid.
4. Hubert Mitchell and Annie Johnson Flint, "He Giveth More Grace" © 1941, renewed 1969 by Lillenas Publishing Company. Used by Permission. *Hymns of Faith and Life,* (Winona Lake, Ind.: Light and Life Press and the Wesley Press, 1976).